A COMPANION
TO THE
MERCERSBURG
THEOLOGY

CASCADE COMPANIONS

The Christian theological tradition provides an embarrassment of riches: from Scripture to modern scholarship, we are blessed with a vast and complex theological inheritance. And yet this feast of traditional riches is too frequently inaccessible to the general reader.

The Cascade Companions series addresses the challenge by publishing books that combine academic rigor with broad appeal and readability. They aim to introduce nonspecialist readers to that vital storehouse of authors, documents, themes, histories, arguments, and movements that comprise this heritage with brief yet compelling volumes.

RECENT TITLES IN THIS SERIES:

A COMPANION TO THE MERCERSBURG THEOLOGY

Evangelical Catholicism in the Mid-Nineteenth Century

WILLIAM B. EVANS

 CASCADE *Books* · Eugene, Oregon

A COMPANION TO THE MERCERSBURG THEOLOGY
Evangelical Catholicism in the Mid-Nineteenth Century

Cascade Companions 44

Cascade Books
An Imprint of Wipf and Stock Publishers
199 W. 8th Ave., Suite 3
Eugene, OR 97401

www.wipfandstock.com

PAPERBACK ISBN: 978-1-4982-0744-7
HARDCOVER ISBN: 978-1-4982-0746-1
EBOOK ISBN: 978-1-4982-0745-4

Cataloging-in-Publication data:

Names: Evans, William B., author.

Title: A Companion to Mercersburg Theology / William B. Evans.

Description: Eugene, OR: Cascade Books, 2019. | Cascade Companions 44. | Includes bibliographical references and index.

Identifiers: ISBN: 978-1-4982-0744-7 (paperback). | ISBN: 978-1-4982-0746-1 (hardcover). | ISBN: 978-1-4982-0745-4 (ebook).

Subjects: LCSH: Mercersburg theology. | Theology, Doctrinal. | Reformed Church—United States—Doctrines. | Nevin, John Williamson, 1803–1886. | Schaff, Philip, 1819–1893.

Classification: BX9571 E93 2019 (print). | BX9571 (epub).

Manufactured in the U.S.A.   04/10/19

To Andrew David and Stefanie Evans,
who have grown to love the Church

CONTENTS

ACKNOWLEDGMENTS

THROUGH THEIR STRATEGIC REPRINTS of key materials and their publication of the Mercersburg Theology Study Series, the publisher of this volume, Wipf and Stock, has played a distinct and important role in the current resurgence of interest in the Mercersburg Theology. The expertise of the editorial and production staffs and their patience with an author who asked for a deadline extension or two are much appreciated.

Special thanks are also due to the community of scholars who have worked in recent decades on Mercersburg topics. Here I must mention my editorial colleagues in the ongoing Mercersburg Theology Study Series (MTSS): W. Bradford Littlejohn, David W. Layman, Linden J. DeBie, David Bains, Theodore L. Trost, and Lee C. Barrett. David Layman was kind enough to read the manuscript, though I hasten to add that he is not responsible for any mistakes and infelicities in the finished product. Theologians and historians—especially Lee Barrett, Anne Thayer, and Peter Schmiechen—connected with Lancaster Theological Seminary, the successor institution to Mercersburg, have played an instrumental role in furthering research on

Mercersburg. In addition, the officers and membership of the Mercersburg Society have done much to keep the flame alive through their annual Mercersburg Convocations at Lancaster Theological Seminary and financial support of publication projects. In fact, some of the interpretations in this volume were earlier presented at Convocation meetings.

The librarians at the McCain Library of Erskine College in Due West, South Carolina, have been most helpful in accessing scarce nineteenth-century materials from their own and other collections. And, of course, the archives of the Evangelical and Reformed Historical Society housed in the Philip Schaff Library at Lancaster Theological Seminary in Lancaster, Pennsylvania continue to be an essential resource for in-depth research on the Mercersburg Theology.

Lastly, special thanks are due to my wife Fay, a fellow teacher whose literary interests in nineteenth-century Britain have enriched our lives together, and whose encouragement has helped to make this volume possible.

INTRODUCTION

THIS COMPANION TO THE Mercersburg Theology is, in keeping with the series aims, a brief introduction to a mid-nineteenth-century theological movement named after the small Pennsylvania town that housed the theological seminary where the principle figures taught. On the face of it, the late twentieth- and early twenty-first-century revival of interest in the theology of John Williamson Nevin, Philip Schaff, and their students is more than a bit surprising, and a key concern of this volume is not only to facilitate understanding of the Mercersburg Theology in its own historical context, but also to engage the reasons for this more recent interest in it.

In their own nineteenth-century context, Nevin and Schaff were swimming against the stream of the prevailing American religious and theological culture with its revivalism, rationalism, individualism, and denominationalism. They worked in the tiny town of Mercersburg in south-central Pennsylvania some forty miles from Gettysburg, far from the urban intellectual centers of the day. Moreover, the theological seminary in Mercersburg was affiliated with the small immigrant German Reformed Church that lacked many of the financial and intellectual resources enjoyed by more established American denominations. In contrast to the philosophical tradition of British empiricism, especially as it was codified in the Scottish Common Sense Realism dominant in America for much of the nineteenth century, the Mercersburg thinkers looked to idealist currents of thought, and especially to the speculative idealism of Germany—ways of thinking that seemed alien to most Americans at that time and are certainly regarded by many as outdated today.

Nevertheless, despite these challenges the Mercersburg thinkers "punched above their weight." They interacted with many of the leading theologians of their day, not only in America but also in Britain and the Continent. They were also deeply engaged in a heady three-way American conversation with the New England Congregational Calvinists to the north and the Princeton Seminary Presbyterians to the east over the nature and shape of the Reformed theological tradition. In fact, Nevin and Schaff provided a substantive alternative to the evangelical moralism of New England and the predestinarian scholasticism of Princeton. Moreover, they called attention to matters that were largely ignored in the American church context—the centrality of the Incarnation, the importance of the church as the people of God and sphere of salvation, the sacraments as objectively real means of grace rather than bare signs and mere mental acts of remembrance, and the importance of liturgical worship that proclaimed and mediated these objective realities to the faithful. To the extent that such issues continue to generate interest and attention, the Mercersburg theologians have something substantial and relevant to say.

The German Reformed Theological Seminary at Mercersburg was established in 1825, one of many ecclesiastically affiliated theological seminaries to emerge in nineteenth-century America. Before this period, the college or university liberal-arts degree, with its training in classics, was the requisite preparation for ordained ministry in Protestant churches; but by the latter part of the eighteenth century some pastors began to welcome theological students into their homes. A few of these were officially designated as theological professors of their denominations, but this model of theological education was not a permanent solution. The theological curriculum was becoming more complex, and one individual taken up with pastoral duties as well as theological instruction was increasingly unable to keep up. In addition, churches wanted to preserve and perpetuate their theological distinctives in the context of the emerging American denominational marketplace, and such causes needed trained and articulate proponents.[1] Thus it is not surprising that beginning in the first decade of the nineteenth-century theological seminaries began to emerge in America—Andover in Massachusetts (Congregationalist, 1808), Princeton in New Jersey (Presbyterian, 1812), General in New York (Episcopalian, 1817), Pittsburgh in Pennsylvania (Associate Reformed, 1818), Auburn (Presbyterian, 1820), Union in Virginia (Presbyterian, 1823), Western in Pennsylvania (Presbyterian, 1825), Mercersburg in Pennsylvania (German Reformed, 1825), Gettysburg in Pennsylvania (Lutheran, 1826), Erskine in South Carolina (Associate Reformed, 1837), and so forth.

The German Reformed Seminary was located initially in Carlisle, Pennsylvania, and housed in the facilities of Dickenson College. It was moved to the nearby city of York in 1829, and then to the town of Mercersburg in 1837 (the Seminary moved to its current location in Lancaster,

1. On the reasons for the emergence of theological seminaries, see Miller, *Piety and Intellect*; McCloy, "Founding of Protestant Theological Seminaries."

Pennsylvania, in 1871). Money was tight, and at first a single theological professor, Lewis Mayer, taught the classes. Of great significance, however, was the arrival at the school of Friedrich Augustus Rauch from Germany in 1832, who taught biblical literature and church history at the Seminary and who was instrumental in introducing Hegelian idealist philosophy to America.

Rauch died suddenly in 1841, but he had been joined at the Seminary by John Williamson Nevin in 1840. A native of southeastern Pennsylvania and a graduate of Princeton Theological Seminary, Nevin had taught biblical literature at the Presbyterian Western Theological Seminary for ten years before being recruited by representatives of the German Reformed Synod to teach theology at Mercersburg. Already familiar with German theological scholarship upon his arrival at Mercersburg, Nevin was to become, more than anyone else, the catalyst and theologian of the Mercersburg Theology movement.

Nevin was joined at Mercersburg by Philip Schaff in 1844, who had been recruited from Germany by Synod representatives to teach biblical literature and church history at the seminary. Despite their differing backgrounds—Nevin the Scots-Irish Presbyterian and Schaff the product of both Continental German Reformed and Lutheran influences— the two men quickly found that they shared a remarkably similar theological perspective on the issues of the day. Both were steeped in the Christocentric theology of the German mediating theologians and in German idealism. Both were deeply concerned to do justice to the reality of the church as organic, corporate, and objective reality rather than as merely the aggregate or sum total of individual Christians. Both were convinced that history is governed by the unfolding of ideal reality, and that the entirety of church history— the early and medieval church as well as the Reformation and modern—is therefore significant. Both insisted that the unity of the church throughout history is theologically important, a conviction that informed the nascent ecumenism of the Mercersburg movement. Needless to say, the chaos of the various denominations and sects that they confronted in nineteenth-century America was disturbing to both.

Such ideas were strange to many, both inside and outside the German Reformed Church, and Nevin and Schaff soon found themselves involved in controversy. Truth be told, they did not shy away from debate, and Nevin in particular was a formidable theological controversialist. Nevin's critique of Second Great Awakening revivalism, *The Anxious Bench* (first published in 1843 and again in a much expanded second edition in 1844) was a stringent attack on Finneyite revivalist methods and the conversionist theology that undergirded them. Schaff's inaugural lecture, published as *The Principle of Protestantism*, argued against the apostasy theory (the then-popular notion that the true church dissolved into catholic darkness after the death of the apostles only to be rediscovered by Martin Luther in the sixteenth century) and for a higher appraisal of Roman Catholicism. Schaff went so far as to argue that the church of the future must bring together the best qualities of Rome and Protestantism, and, not surprisingly, he was almost immediately condemned by some in the German Reformed Church as a Romanizer.

Nevin's *The Mystical Presence* was published in 1846 and argued on biblical, theological, and historical grounds for a recovery of John Calvin's doctrine of the real presence of Christ's incarnate humanity in the Lord's Supper. Such Eucharistic ideas, however, stood in considerable tension with the Zwinglian memorialism that prevailed in much of American Protestantism, and again the charges of Romanizing came from Mercersburg's opponents both inside and outside the German Reformed Church.[2] Nevin's debate with Charles Hodge of Princeton on this topic was especially substantive and memorable—a clash of titans, if you will—and many historians believe that Nevin won the debate by a considerable margin.

In 1849 the *Mercersburg Review* was founded as a venue for Nevin and Schaff's literary efforts. Nevin's whirlwind of literary activity continued—he had thirteen articles in the first volume (1849), eleven in the second (1850), ten in the third (1851), and thirteen in the fourth (1852). His evolving theological interests are also evident in these first four volumes of the *Review*. Early on, his work focused especially on the importance of the Apostles' Creed and on the dangers of sectarian Protestantism. Then attention shifts to Christology (especially to the question of whether the Incarnation would have occurred even apart from the Fall), and to the history of the early church as Nevin was pondering the discontinuity of the Protestantism of his day with early Christianity and considering the claims of Rome.

The dramatic break in Nevin's literary activity after the 1852 volume of the *Mercersburg Review* reflects his personal struggles. Physically worn out by his herculean literary efforts and his teaching and administrative labors at the Seminary and Marshall College, and haunted by the possibility that the Protestant experiment was irreparably flawed, he entered the period that became known as "Nevin's Dizziness." Reflective of this, the 1853 volume of the *Review* was reduced from six issues to four, and renamed *The Mercersburg Quarterly Review*.

Nevin's contributions would be more occasional from this point on, but students of Rauch, Nevin, and Schaff—particularly E. V. Gerhart, Henry Harbaugh, Daniel Gans,

2. Mercersburg's relationship to the Reformation is complex. See Evans, "Mercersburg and the Reformation."

and Theodore Apple—were carrying the distinctive Mercersburg perspective forward in the *Review*. Schaff's contributions also became more numerous as his facility with the English language improved, and his fruitful research into the history of the early church continued. By this point, however, the initial burst of theological creativity had subsided, though the task of systematizing the Mercersburg theology, undertaken most notably by E. V. Gerhart (whose *Institutes of the Christian Religion* remains the most complete and systematic presentation of the Mercersburg theology), remained. Also, a major focus of the 1850s and 1860s was generating liturgical resources for the German Reformed Church that reflected the insights and ethos of Mercersburg.

Though the liturgical sensibilities of Mercersburg continued to be influential in many German Reformed congregations, the distinctive theological agenda of Mercersburg began to fade from memory. The concerns of post-Civil War America as it dealt with the pressures of rapid urbanization and massive immigration were quite different from the antebellum period. In Germany, the neo-Kantian moralistic theology of Albrecht Ritschl and his successors displaced the concerns of Schleiermacher and Hegel, and soon this classical Protestant liberalism was being imported into the United States and helping to generate, a bit later, the Social Gospel movement. This new theology was basically naturalistic and moralistic, and the Mercersburg theology—with its christological focus on Incarnation and resurrection, and its ecclesial regard for the church as a supernatural organism—seemed dated. Evidence of this eclipse even within the German Reformed Church is found in an extended 1912 article ("The Mercersburg Theology Historically Considered") by Lancaster Theological Seminary church historian George Warren Richards, who contended that "the formulas of the Mercersburg school are no longer pertinent and adequate," and that "the Mercersburg system has 'had its day and ceased to be.'" The continuing significance of the movement, he suggested, lay in the way that Nevin and Schaff "paved the way for a transition from Puritanism to Modernism."[3]

After the First World War, the dialectical theology of Karl Barth and others emerged. But once again, the Mercersburg theology seemed out of touch with popular trends. Whereas Mercersburg had enthusiastically embraced historical consciousness and scholarship, Barth sought to flee from the acids of historical criticism by locating vital Christian truth in the realm of "suprahistory" where it could not be proven or disproven by historical inquiry. Doubtless Mercersburg's regard for Friedrich Schleiermacher, Barth's *bête noire*, was an embarrassment as well. Finally, Mercersburg's high ecclesiology with its concern for sacramental efficacy and view of the church as the sphere of salvation did not mesh well with Barth's low-church, Zwinglian sensibilities.

But even during the heyday of Dialectical Theology, the stage was being set for a revival of interest in Mercersburg. Initially, this was driven primarily by two developments. First, the mid-twentieth century was the highpoint of the ecumenical movement. Ironically in light of his dismissal of Mercersburg as a vital form of theology some four decades earlier, the same George Warren Richards noted the similarities between the ecumenism of Nevin and Schaff and the pronouncements of the great 1937 ecumenical meetings at Oxford and Edinburgh, and he allowed that "Schaff and Nevin were far-sighted men who had at least

3. Richards, "Mercersburg Theology Historically Considered," 147–48.

a spark of prophecy in their theology."[4] Second, there was the twentieth-century Liturgical Renewal Movement that spilled over from Roman Catholicism into various Protestant denominations. Again, the remarkable similarities to Mercersburg were apparent—liturgical-renewal scholars drew heavily on the worship traditions of the early church, just as Nevin and Schaff had done a century earlier.

So it was that articles and books started to appear praising Nevin and Schaff as theologians of enduring significance and suggesting that the Mercersburg thinkers had something of value to say to the contemporary church. For example, Scott Francis Brenner wrote these effusive words in 1955: "The meeting of Schaff and Nevin was like the concurrence of two heavenly bodies of the first magnitude. The splendor which ensued is known as the Mercersburg Theology, for these two intellectual giants of the Presbyterian-Reformed household of faith wrought out a theological system of singular boldness, relevant to its time, distinctively ecumenical, and of unquestioned enduring worth. I would hazard the assertion that no other American theologians with the exception of Jonathan Edwards and possibly Reinhold Niebuhr have wrought so creatively as Nevin and Schaff."[5]

Suddenly Mercersburg was on the radar screen of theological scholarship. Doctoral dissertations began to be written on Mercersburg topics.[6] But particularly significant were the lectures presented at Austin Presbyterian Theolog-

4. Richards, "Mercersburg Theology—Its Purpose and Principles," 53.

5. Brenner, "Nevin and the Mercersburg Theology," 51.

6. See, e.g., Plummer, "The Theology of John Williamson Nevin in the Mercersburg Period, 1840–1852"; Carlough, "Historical Comparison of the Theology of John Williamson Nevin and Contemporary Protestant Sacramentalism."

ical Seminary in 1960 by the University of Chicago church historian James Hastings Nichols that were published in 1961 as *Romanticism in American Theology: Nevin and Schaff at Mercersburg*. Nichols' volume provided the first extended scholarly analysis of the Mercersburg Theology, and he opined that Nevin and Schaff were "major prophets of the twentieth-century ecumenical movement," adding that "they ranked easily among the first half-dozen American theologians of their generation, along with Charles Hodge, Henry B. Smith, E. A. Park, Horace Bushnell. From the viewpoint of the mid-twentieth century Nevin and Schaff may even seem to be the most relevant of the group."[7]

But many of the Mercersburg writings were long out of print or found only in the musty pages of the *Mercersburg Review*. In other words, accessibility of texts was a real problem, and so beginning in the early 1960s there were concerted efforts to republish some of the more significant Mercersburg writings. Nevin's originally serialized autobiography, *My Own Life*, was published by the Historical Society of the Evangelical and Reformed Church in 1964. Schaff's *The Principle of Protestantism* and a collection of Nevin's *The Mystical Presence and Other Writings on the Eucharist* appeared in the never-completed Lancaster Series on the Mercersburg Theology in 1964 and 1966 respectively. James Hastings Nichols also edited an anthology, *The Mercersburg Theology*, that collected key Mercersburg texts on the topics of the church, Christology, the sacraments, ministry, and human freedom that appeared in 1966. Significant anthologies of writings by Nevin and Schaff edited by Charles Yrigoyen, Jr. and George M. Bricker appeared in 1978 and 1979, the Nevin collection appropriately titled *Catholic and Reformed* and the Schaff volume *Reformed and Catholic*. Most recently, in what promises to be the most

7. Nichols, *Romanticism in American Theology*, 3–4.

complete project to date, volumes in the Mercersburg Theology Study Series (MTSS) began appearing in 2012 (where possible, citations in this volume are keyed to this series).

A second important source of interest in the Mercersburg Theology must be noted in this Introduction—American Evangelicalism. Though the Christian's vital experience of salvation was important to both of them, Nevin and Schaff were roundly critical of the revivalist excesses, rampant subjectivity, low sacramentology, historical amnesia, and lack of liturgical sensibility that characterized much of the American Protestant Evangelicalism of their day. These traits that Mercersburg found so troubling are still very much present in American Evangelicalism today, and more than a few late twentieth- and twenty-first-century Evangelicals have found in Mercersburg an antidote to them. Some of these have come from the Presbyterian and Reformed wing of Evangelicalism, and they have found in Mercersburg a substantial alternative model of the Reformed tradition.

Thus the contemporary revival of interest in the Mercersburg Theology has brought together a remarkably broad spectrum of Christians—from members of liberal mainline denominations interested in ecumenism and liturgical renewal to Evangelicals seeking a deeper and more historically informed experience of the Christian faith. Reflecting on the formation of a society devoted to the discussion and preservation of Mercersburg distinctives, liturgical scholar Howard Hageman wrote in 1985: "The larger majority of those present were working pastors (and some laypeople) who are uneasy about the integrity of the Reformed tradition in today's America. Repelled by the sterility of a fossilized Calvinism, appalled by the success of a mindless evangelicalism, and discouraged by the emptiness of classic liberalism, they are looking for a fresh understanding of the Reformed tradition. Mercersburg, with its emphasis on Incarnation, church, sacraments, and ministry as essential elements of that tradition, seems to offer at least an interesting possibility."[8] Could it be that Mercersburg's "Evangelical Catholicism" is as salient and intriguing today as it was in the time of Nevin and Schaff?

8. Hageman, "Back to Mercersburg," 6.

1

DRAMATIS PERSONNAE

A THEOLOGICAL MOVEMENT AS distinctive in its nineteenth-century American context as the Mercersburg
Theology was, not surprisingly, produced by some equally
distinctive and intriguing personalities. Because this volume is intended as a brief introduction we will focus here
on the four individuals most directly involved in shaping
the Mercersburg theological movement—the philologist
and philosopher Friedrich Autustus Rauch, the primary
theologian of the movement John Williamson Nevin, historian and biblical scholar Philip Schaff, and finally, the
most prominent student of these three, E. V. Gerhart, who
produced the only full-fledged systematic theology in the
Mercersburg tradition.

As we consider these important figures, it is useful to reflect on both the brevity and periodization of the
movement. The truly creative period of the Mercersburg

Theology lasted less than two decades—from Nevin's sermon on "Catholic Unity" and the second edition of *The Anxious Bench* in 1844 until Schaff's departure for New York in 1863, though the ecclesial, sacramental, and liturgical implications continued to be explored and worked out for decades by their students such as Emanuel V. Gerhart.

Casting his chronological net more broadly, Gerhart's periodization of the movement helps us to grasp something of its evolution and shifting foci. He suggested that the Mercersburg "movement had three phases. The first was philosophical (1836–43); the second was theological, and turned chiefly on the church question (1843–58); the third was liturgical (1858–66)."[1] During Gerhart's first period the key figure is F. A. Rauch; during the second John W. Nevin was clearly the most forceful and influential figure, and during the third Philip Schaff with his prodigious knowledge of liturgical history came to the fore.

FRIEDRICH AUGUSTUS RAUCH

The most personally enigmatic of the four, Friedrich Augustus Rauch was born on July 22, 1806, in Kirchbracht, a town in what was then the German principality of Electoral Hesse.[2] On both sides of his family, Rauch was connected to the Reformed Church—his father Heinrich was the German Reformed pastor in Kirchbracht and his maternal grandfather was a Reformed pastor as well. After receiving his secondary education at *Gymnasia* in Hanau and Büdingen, Rauch enrolled at the University of Giessen

---

1. Gerhart, "Mercersburg Theology," 311.

2. Biographical treatments of Rauch include Nevin, *Eulogy on the Life and Character of Frederick Augustus Rauch*; and Ziegler, *Frederick Augustus Rauch*. The material in this section is largely based on Ziegler's account.

in 1824, where he excelled in studies of the Greek and Roman writers of classical antiquity. Desirous of an academic career and needing the terminal degree, Rauch received his doctorate from the University of Marburg for a dissertation on the play *Electra*, by the fifth-century BCE Greek poet Sophocles ("In Sophoclis Electram Observationes"). But Rauch's interests now turned to philosophy, and he came under the influence of the right-wing Hegelian Karl Daub, then teaching at Heidelberg. Thereafter, Rauch's work would bear a distinctly Hegelian stamp.

With doctorate in hand, the ambitious Rauch now earnestly sought an academic post in Germany, and here the story becomes murky. Nevin would later claim that Rauch had been a protégé of Karl Daub, that he was appointed to a professorial position at the University of Heidelberg, but that he left the country after his lectures aroused political suspicions.[3] Rauch may have encouraged such sentiments, but, as the carefully researched biography of Rauch by Howard Ziegler reveals, the true situation was rather different.[4] In late 1828 he returned to the University of Giessen, where he was provisionally appointed as a *Privatdocent* (a teacher with official standing at the University whose income came directly from student fees rather than a salary

3. Nevin, "Preliminary Notice to the Second Edition," in Rauch, *Psychology*, vii, wrote: "Daub had fixed his eye upon him as a young man of more than common promise, who might be expected to do good service to the cause of science, in the department to which he wished to consecrate his life. On quitting Heidelberg, he spent a year again at Giessen, as *professor extraordinarius*; at the end of which time, he received an appointment to a regular professorship at Heidelberg. Here however his fair prospects were suddenly covered with a dark cloud. In his lectures, he was supposed to have expressed himself with too much freedom with regard to government. Jealousy was awakened; and it was considered necessary, in the judgment of his friends, that he should quit the country."

4. See Ziegler, *Friedrich Augustus Rauch*, 10–17.

from the school). Soon, however, Rauch became embroiled in a personal dispute with a senior faculty member in his academic department. He filed a lawsuit which dragged on for well over a year, and this public conflict seriously reduced Rauch's chances of ever having a successful academic career in Germany. And so he decided to emigrate to America in 1831.

Arriving in New York, Rauch then journeyed to the German immigrant communities of southeastern Pennsylvania. Settling in the town of Easton, Rauch quickly learned English, taught music, and was named Professor of German at the fledgling Lafayette College in 1832. Almost immediately, however, Rauch resigned to accept a dual appointment at the Classical School (soon to become Marshall College) and as professor of biblical literature at the Theological Seminary of the German Reformed Church in York, Pennsylvania. Both schools were soon transferred to the town of Mercersburg, where Rauch taught in the seminary and assumed the presidency of Marshall College. The original seminary professor, Lewis Mayer, resigned in 1839 and Rauch was left as the sole professor. This situation was remedied in 1840, when John Williamson Nevin was called as Professor of Theology to replace Mayer. Their collegial relationship was to last less than a year, however, for Rauch died suddenly on March 2, 1841.

Rauch's significance for the Mercersburg Theology requires some explanation. Key Mercersburg emphases—the Christocentric character of theology, the sacraments as real means of grace, the organic historical development of the church as the objective locus of salvation—are largely absent from Rauch's work.[5] What Rauch provided, however, was an informed presentation of German idealism in the Hegelian tradition that subsequently served as a

5. See Nichols, *Romanticism in American Theology*, 48.

philosophical idiom for the Mercersburg theological formulations. The key text is Rauch's *Psychology: or, A View of the Human Soul*, initially published in 1840 and again in a second edition in 1841, which was, as is often noted, the first systematic presentation of the Hegelian philosophy of mind in America. Here he affirmed the priority of the universal over the particular, the organic nature of life as constituted by a "plastic power" or life principle, an integrative view of the human person in which body and soul are expressions of this deeper life principle, and the foundational role of self-consciousness for human identity—themes that were to resonate deeply in the Mercersburg Theology.

JOHN WILLIAMSON NEVIN

Southeastern Pennsylvania was home, not only to immigrant Germans, but also to large numbers of Presbyterian Scots-Irish. Nevin's grandfather had journeyed from Ulster to the new world. His father, John Nevin, was a graduate of nearby Dickenson College and a gentleman farmer in Franklin County, Pennsylvania, who married Martha Mc-Cracken. Nevin's grandmother on his father's side was of English extraction and a sister of Hugh Willliamson, the prominent physician, scholar, politician, and delegate from North Carolina to the American Constitutional Convention.[6] Into this respectable family John Williamson Nevin was born in 1803; the origins of his given name and his Presbyterian roots are clear enough. He came from "good stock," and he knew it—his patrician demeanor and somewhat elitist attitudes are explainable in part by this personal background.

6. For biographical information, see Appel, *Life and Work of John Williamson Nevin*; Nevin, *My Own Life*; Hart, *John Williamson Nevin: High Church Calvinist*; Wentz, *John Williamson Nevin*.

Nevin's religious upbringing in the Middle Spring Presbyterian Church near Shippensburg, Pennsylvania, was of the older Presbyterian style—focused on the nurture of congregants through the preaching of the word, the sacraments, and careful religious instruction. As Nevin himself tells it, "the old Presbyterian faith, into which I was born, was based throughout on the idea of covenant family religion, church membership by God's holy act in baptism, and following this a regular catechetical training of the young, with direct reference to their coming to the Lord's table. In one word, all proceeded on the theory of sacramental, educational religion, as it had belonged properly to all the national branches of the Reformed Church in Europe from the beginning."[7]

Nevin was prepared in Latin and Greek for college by his father and entered Union College in Schenectady, New York, in 1817. Union was a cooperative venture of New England Congregationalist and Presbyterian interests, and there Nevin encountered the revivalist tradition of the Second Great Awakening successors of Jonathan Edwards for the first time. During a visit to the College by the Connecticut Congregationalist evangelist Asahel Nettleton, Nevin himself had a conversion experience of sorts. His later evaluation of the experience was ambivalent; while he did not completely discount the value of this religious awakening, he also later spoke of the Union faculty members and students who were seeking to bring others to the "new birth" as "miserable obstetricians." But the contrast between the nurture model piety of his upbringing and revivalism was stark—on the nurture model the sacraments and catechetical instruction counted for much and transient emotional experience counted for little; on the conversionist model training and nurture in the faith counted for little and vivid

7. Nevin, *My Own Life*, 2.

emotional experience much.[8] Furthermore, Nevin's natural tendency toward introspection was apparently exacerbated by the relentless subjectivity of revivalist piety; it was, after all, the business of itinerant evangelists to disquiet rather than to comfort their hearers, and the combination precipitated an extended period of nervous exhaustion. We also must not discount the importance of these religious encounters for Nevin's later theological career; Union College was Nevin's first exposure to revivalistic "Puritanism," and both his later critique of it and his preference for Christian nurture and the churchly objectivity of the sacraments doubtless must be seen in light of these painful experiences.

After a period of convalescence, Nevin enrolled at Princeton Theological Seminary, then entering its second decade of existence. He excelled in the study of biblical Hebrew, and such was his skill that upon graduation he was called to substitute for Charles Hodge in the school's Department of Oriental and Biblical Literature during the latter's two-year sojourn at the universities of Europe. While teaching at Princeton Seminary, Nevin wrote a widely circulated two-volume textbook on biblical backgrounds entitled *A Summary of Biblical Antiquities; for the Use of Sunday School Teachers and for the Benefit of Families.*

Nevertheless, Nevin's spiritual struggles over assurance of salvation continued. Princeton was the flagship seminary of the Presbyterian Church with roots in the eighteenth-century pro-Great Awakening New Side, and the teaching there reflected both the older nurture piety of Reformed orthodoxy and the increasingly popular conversionist Awakening tradition, and once again Nevin felt himself caught between two dissimilar modes of religion. He wrote: "There were in fact two different theories or schemes

8. On the contrast between these two models of piety, see Evans, "Tale of Two Pieties."

of piety at work in my mind, which refused to coalesce. One was the New England Puritanic theory, as it had taken possession particularly of the revival system, which was now assuming to be the only true sense of the Gospel all over the country; the other was the old proper Presbyterian theory of the seventeenth century . . . There was, for me, a difference between the two systems, which I could feel without being able to explain . . . Our teaching [at Princeton] was not steadily and consistently in one direction."[9]

When Hodge returned from his studies in Europe, Nevin was called at the age of 27 to teach at a new Presbyterian school, Western Theological Seminary, near Pittsburgh that was founded to provide theological education for what was then the western frontier (though even as it began the frontier had moved further west). There Nevin was busy—teaching his classes, providing pulpit supply to rural churches, and editing a moral-reform magazine. He also married Martha Jenkins of Lancaster on New Year's Day of 1835, and was finally ordained to the gospel ministry in the Presbyterian Church. But more important for our story here is the research and reading he conducted during this period.

Nevin had long had an affinity for seventeenth-century devotional writers of a mystical and Platonizing bent such as the Puritan John Howe and Archbishop Robert Leighton. With his biblical-studies teaching responsibilities at Western Seminary, Nevin began to explore German exegetical literature, but even more important was his growing interest in church history. His church history classes at Princeton had been disappointing. As Nevin later put it, "It was, for me, still a system only of dead outward facts. I had no

9. Nevin, *My Own Life*, 22–23. For a subtle reading of the religious context at Princeton Seminary during this period, see Loetscher, *Facing the Enlightenment and Pietism*.

sense of its constitutional relation everywhere to the inmost significance of these facts themselves."[10] While at Western he learned about the idealist historiography of the German church historian August Neander (1789–1850), and he began to study the German language so that he could read Neander for himself. Here he encountered a view of history as the organic unfolding of great ideas and impulses, a unified narrative moving toward its God-appointed goal. Neander's impact on Nevin was electric: "He caused church history to become for me like the creations of poetry and romance. How much I owe to him in the way of excitement, impulse, suggestion, knowledge, both literary and religious, reaching onward into all my later life, is more than I can pretend to explain, for it is in truth more than I have power to understand."[11]

Thus when Nevin was called to teach at Mercersburg in 1840, he was already familiar with German theological scholarship. There he found Rauch's idealism to be agreeable with his own Platonizing sensibilities and historiographical interests. With the arrival of Philip Schaff in 1844, Nevin gained a learned colleague whose scholarly and theological interests complemented his own.

Despite the heavy teaching and administrative load that fell on Nevin after Rauch's death in 1841, he quickly sought to address what he saw as the needs of his new church. In particular, he noted the growing influence of seminal revivalist Charles Grandison Finney's "New Measures" revivalism in the German Reformed Church. Finney argued that revivals of religion are not miraculous, but rather are simply "a purely philosophical result of the right use of the constituted means—as much so as any other

10. Nevin, *My Own Life*, 40.

11. Ibid., 139.

effect produced by the application of means."[12] In other words, revivals occur whenever the appropriate techniques are utilized. Finney's apparent success spawned a host of imitators, but Nevin was troubled by the individualism and psychological manipulation of the approach. He penned *The Anxious Bench*, first published in 1843, and again in a much-expanded second edition in 1844. The 1844 edition was, in addition to being an astringent critique of revivalist theory and praxis, the first cogent statement of an alternative that has come to be known as the Mercersburg Theology. Here the crucial themes of organic union with Christ, the generic humanity of the first and second Adams, the mediation of the church, and the priority of the general over the particular all come to expression.

Revivalism assumed that the point of entry into the Christian life was the individual's conversion experience rather than baptism, a perspective that had little use for the sacraments and implied that the church was simply the sum total of those who have had this particular sort of experience. Moreover, American Protestantism in general viewed the idea that the sacraments might actually do something as incipient Catholicism, and the notion that Christ is somehow truly present in the Lord's Supper as verging on the Roman Catholic doctrine of transubstantiation. In 1846, Nevin's best-known theological treatise—*The Mystical Presence: A Vindication of the Reformed or Calvinistic Doctrine of the Holy Eucharist*—was published. The book was an exposition of the traditional Reformed doctrine of the true presence of Christ's incarnate humanity in the Supper as found in Calvin and the Reformed confessions, and provocatively drew attention to the way that the "modern Puritan theory" of Nevin's New England Calvinist and Presbyterian contemporaries diverged from it.

12. Finney, *Lectures on Revivals of Religion*, 12.

With the launching of *The Mercersburg Review* in 1849, Nevin's attention turned to what he often termed "the church question." He critiqued the sectarian impulse endemic in American Protestantism and explored the relationship between Christology and ecclesiology. But Nevin's sustained critique of the popular Protestantism of his day as individualistic, sectarian, and unsacramental posed an obvious, if implicit, question: might Rome be right after all? In 1851 Nevin entered a period of ecclesial uncertainty, which contemporaries called "Nevin's Dizziness," and he ceased teaching at the Seminary in 1852. By 1854, however, Nevin had definitively decided to remain within the Reformed and Protestant camp. At the end of the day, he probably realized that Roman Catholicism, though different, represented a fundamental challenge to his theological convictions as serious as popular Protestantism. He resumed his involvement in the German Reformed Church, was a member of a committee that produced a new liturgy for the church, and served as the President of Marshall College in Lancaster from 1866 until his retirement a decade later. The last decade of his life was spent in quiet retirement at his home in Lancaster, and he died on June 6, 1886 at the age of 84.

PHILIP SCHAFF

Nevin, who had taught the seminary curriculum by himself since Rauch's death in 1841, was doubtless delighted when Philip Schaff arrived to take up his teaching duties at Mercersburg. It is difficult to imagine a better qualified replacement for Rauch than Schaff and, unlike Nevin, the scope of scholarly Schaff's work and influence was to extend far beyond the confines of the German Reformed Church.[13]

13. Biographical treatments include David Schaff, *Life of Philip Schaff*; Shriver, *Philip Schaff*.

Hailing from the German-speaking portion of Switzerland, Schaff was born in the town of Chur on January 1, 1819. He was effectively orphaned after his father died while Philip was an infant, for when his mother remarried Philip was placed in an orphanage. That he was able to rise above such humble and straightened circumstances is a tribute to his intelligence and hard work. Well-placed individuals took an interest in the gifted Schaff and off he went to Germany for his education. He attended a school associated with the Württemberg pietist movement where he experienced a religious awakening, and received his secondary education at a *Gymnasium* (in the German educational system, an advanced secondary school that prepared the student for university) in Stuttgart.

As was then the custom, Schaff's university years were spent at multiple institutions and he was able to sit under many of the leading theologians in Germany. At Tübingen he studied under the Hegelian New Testament scholar Ferdinand Christian Baur (1792–1860), whose dialectical theory of Christian origins was provoking much discussion, the Lutheran exegete Christian Friedrich Schmid (1794–1852), and the brilliant mediating theologian Isaak August Dorner (1809–1884). At Halle Schaff came under the influence of preacher and theologian F. A. G. Tholuck (1799–1877), who reinforced his pietist tendencies, and theologian Julius Müller (1801–1878), whose monumental multi-volume *The Christian Doctrine of Sin* began to be published the year of Schaff's sojourn in Halle (1839).

The capstone of Schaff's university years, however, was the term he spent at the University of Berlin in 1840. There he listened to the church historian August Neander (1789–1850), whose historiographical influence on Schaff was profound and lasting. In Berlin he also became part of the social circle of the influential exegete, Lutheran

confessionalist, and churchman Ernst Wilhelm Hengstenberg (1802–1869), who furthered Schaff's career and
would later recommend him for the post at Mercersburg.
Closely associated with Hengstenberg were the politically
well-connected Gerlach brothers, Leopold and Ludwig, and
the culturally conservative and churchly sensibilities of this
group left a profound mark on the young Schaff.[14] At Berlin Schaff also heard the philosopher Friedrich Schelling
(1775–1854), whose dialectical view of history anticipated
a Johannine church of the future that would succeed and
transcend the Petrine Christianity of Catholicism and the
Pauline Christianity of Protestantism. As George Shriver
notes, these influences were seminal on the young Schaff:
"In Berlin Schaff began to develop his genius for eclecticism
and synthesis. Baur had suggested organic development,
Neander had both reinforced his piety and instilled the
historian's methodology, and Hengstenberg and Gerlach
had enabled him to ground his concept of the kingdom of
God in the tradition of the visible church. One last major
ingredient was added by F. W. J. Schelling. His lectures on
mythology and revelation gave substance and grandeur to
Schaff's ecumenical vision of a future age of 'evangelical
catholicism.'"[15]

After finishing his term at Berlin in 1840, Schaff wrote
his doctoral dissertation on the topic of the sin against the
Holy Spirit. Upon completion of this project, Schaff trav-
eled the Mediterranean for a time with a wealthy family
whose child he tutored (a job arranged by Hengstenberg)
before beginning work as a *Privatdozent* at the University
of Berlin later in 1842. By all appearances, a bright academic career lay ahead of him in Germany; but in 1843 a
visit from a delegation of the German Reformed Synod in

14. See Nichols, *Romanticism in American Theology*, 64–83.

15. Shriver, *Philip Schaff*, 8–9.

the United States intervened. Wanting to hire a prominent German scholar to teach church history and biblical literature in their seminary at Mercersburg, they were pointed to Schaff. After careful consideration and encouragement from friends, Schaff decided to accept the offer and move to America.

Schaff was ordained to the ministry in the Reformed Church at Elberfeld in April of 1844. The content of the sermon he preached on that occasion, in which he vividly portrayed the German immigrant communities in America as beset by the threats of irreligion, Roman Catholicism, and sectarianism, was deemed unnecessarily critical by some and was to cause him problems when he arrived in the New World. While in transit from Germany to America, Schaff spent six weeks in England meeting with many religious leaders there and improving his skill in the English language.

Upon his arrival in Mercersburg in August of 1844, Schaff was delighted to find that his new colleague, John W. Nevin, was familiar with German scholarship and that they had much in common theologically. His inaugural lecture on "The Principle of Protestantism," was presented on October of 1844 in German and then quickly translated for publication by Nevin. It was a learned *tour de force*, and it created quite a stir. Schaff focused on the centrality of the church question and unpacked the implications of an historiography of organic development, arguing that the church has only gradually come to deeper understanding of important doctrine, that the Protestant Reformation built on the best of the Catholic past, and that further development may be anticipated beyond the Protestantism of Schaff's day. All this was troubling to those who thought in categories of static truth or falsity, and who regarded Roman Catholicism as the great religious and political threat of the day.

Egged on by Philadelphia pastor Joseph Berg, champion of a version of the "apostasy theory" that traced the lineage of the German Reformed Church back through the medieval Waldensians to the Apostles, a resolution critical of Schaff's book was passed by Philadelphia Classis of the German Reformed Church, and a heresy trial took place at the 1845 Synod. Schaff was doubtless relieved when the Synod voted overwhelmingly to vindicate its new professor. Though the next year Schaff also faced questions about his views as to whether those who do not hear the gospel message will have an opportunity for salvation in the afterlife, his position in the German Reformed Church was increasingly secure.

A bachelor when he arrived in America, Schaff married Mary Elizabeth Schley in 1845. The couple had eight children, only three of whom survived to adulthood. The grief of these losses later induced Schaff to write his privately circulated *In Memoriam: Our Children in Heaven* (1876).

Schaff's years at Mercersburg were a time of intense literary activity, and he was hard at work on a succession of volumes that would establish him as a preeminent church historian and theologian in America. For example, a sophisticated introduction to historiography, *What Is Church History: A Vindication of the Idea of Historical Development*, was published in 1846, followed by his *History of the Apostolic Church with a General Introduction to Church History* in 1854. *The Moral Character of Christ, or the Perfection of Christ's Humanity a Proof of His Divinity* appeared in 1861 and sounded Christological themes to which he would return throughout his career. Schaff was also uniquely situated to explain Germany to Americans and America to Germans. His *America: A Sketch of the Political, Social, and Religious Character of the United State of North America* was published in 1855 and based on lectures Schaff presented in Germany in 1854, while *Germany, Its Universities, Theology, and Religion* was published in 1857 and remains an important resource for understanding German theology and institutional religion of that period.

The outbreak of the Civil War in 1861 also helped to bring Schaff's time at Mercersburg to an end. Mercersburg is located north of the Shenandoah Valley in an area that for centuries had served as a route from northeast to southwest. This region was strategically important, and incursions by Confederate soldiers were common. Located less than forty miles from the town of Gettysburg, the Seminary facilities at Mercersburg were commandeered for use as a military hospital to treat the wounded after that decisive battle. These military interruptions, coupled with Schaff's desire to live near the resources of an urban center, caused him to relocate to New York City in 1863, and he submitted his resignation to the Synod two years later.

In New York City Schaff continued his whirlwind of activity, albeit on a much larger stage. From 1865–1870 Schaff served as the Secretary of the New York Sabbath Committee, and he became an ardent advocate of the Puritan Sabbath.[16] In 1870 he accepted an appointment as Professor of Theological Encyclopedia and Christian Symbolism at Union Theological Seminary in New York City. Because Union was affiliated with the Presbyterian Church in the United States of America, Schaff also transferred his ministerial credentials to that body.

As the name of his chair implies, Schaff was free to teach courses in a variety of areas, and his publishing during the Union Seminary period reflects this broad range of interest. A remarkable witness to this encyclopedic knowledge of the field is his *Theological Propaedeutic: A General Introduction to the Study of Theology: Exegetical, Historical,*

16. See Schaff, *The Anglo-American Sabbath.*

Systematic, and Practical (1892). In the area of biblical studies, Schaff edited and contributed to the English translation of the German commentary series of J. P. Lange, and he chaired the American translation committee of the Revised Version of the Bible. He was also instrumental in the formation of the Society of Biblical Literature. But it is in the area of Church History that Schaff's published contributions are most evident and lasting, and his final appointment at Union Seminary was as Professor of Church History. He edited massive collections of patristic literature (*The Ante-Nicene Fathers* and *The Nicene and Post-Nicene Fathers*). *The Schaff-Herzog Encyclopedia of Religious Knowledge* (and its successor *The New Schaff-Herzog Encyclopedia*) provides a comprehensive window on theological scholarship of the period. Schaff's *Creeds of Christendom* and his seven-volume *History of the Christian Church* (the eighth volume was completed by his son David Schaff) stand as monuments to his learning, and he was a founder and first president of the American Society of Church History.

Schaff was also a tireless advocate for cooperation and eventual union between Christian denominations. He was deeply involved in the American wing of the Evangelical Alliance, and helped to organize the great 1873 conference of that organization in New York. Symbolic of this commitment is the fact that his last public act a month before his death on October 20, 1893 was the presentation of an address on "The Reunion of Christendom" at the World's Parliament of Religions in Chicago.

The two great figures of the Mercersburg Theology movement—John Nevin and Philip Schaff—shared many theological commitments but contrasts between them are worthy of mention. The personalities of the two were quite different. Nevin was reserved while Schaff was gregarious. Nevin's propensity for nervous exhaustion and depression is well known, while Schaff was the eternal optimist. Schaff loved to travel—he made fourteen trips to Europe during his American sojourn—while Nevin preferred to stay close to home in southeastern Pennsylvania. Nevin was an avid polemicist while Schaff was irenic; the irony here is that it was Schaff rather than Nevin who faced a formal heresy trial in the German Reformed Church.[17]

In terms of their scholarly inclinations, Nevin was a theologian with a deep interest in history, while Schaff was an historian keenly attuned to the theological implications of historical research. Nevin was a master of the incisive theological essay, while Schaff is better known for his monographs and multi-volume publishing projects.

Perhaps most ironic, however, is the fact that, unlike his American colleague Nevin, the Swiss-German Schaff came to terms with the variegated character of American Christianity. He became a fervent advocate of the American separation of church and state, and he was deeply involved in what has been called the "Evangelical United Front" with its voluntary societies devoted to various moralistic causes such as Sabbath observance and temperance. He embraced the revivalism of D. L. Moody, and he began to distinguish between invidious sects and denominations; the latter, he thought, would be instrumental in the emergence of Christian reunion and a higher Christian synthesis. Schaff's Schelling-influenced eschatological vision of a religious future in which America would play a decisive role is evident:

17. Shriver, *Philip Schaff*, 20, writes: "There were important differences, however, having to do with psychological composition and temperament. Nevin was polemic and bombastic; Schaff was tolerant and irenic. Mood, method, and approach separated these men, but this was not always picked up by outsiders . . . Nevertheless, in their essential attitudes on the church, theology, and history, these two professors were in almost complete agreement."

God has great surprises in store. The Reformation is not by any means the last word He has spoken. We may confidently look and hope for something better than Romanism and Protestantism. And free America, where all the churches are commingling and rivalling with each other, may become the chief theatre of such a reunion of Christendom as will preserve every truly Christian and valuable element in the various types which it has assumed in the course of ages, and make them more effective than they were in their separation and antagonism. The denominational discords will be solved at last in the concord of Christ, the Lord and Saviour of all that love, worship, and follow Him.[18]

EMANUEL VOGEL GERHART

Although E. V. Gerhart is generally regarded as a student of the Mercersburg leaders (he studied under both Rauch and Nevin), in fact he was only a year and a half younger than Schaff, and so he has some claim to being part of the first generation. In light of Rauch's early death, Nevin's departure from Mercersburg and later preoccupation with administrative matters, and Schaff's departure for Presbyterianism, it fell to Gerhart to produce a systematic treatment of the Mercersburg Theology.

The son of an immigrant German Reformed pastor, Gerhart was born on June 13, 1817, in the central Pennsylvania town of Freeburg.[19] The German language he learned

18. Schaff, *Church and State in the United States*, 83; quoted in Shriver, *Philip Schaff*, 41. The most complete study of Schaff's evolving interpretation of American Christianity is Graham, *Cosmos in the Chaos*.

19. Biographical treatments of Gerhart's life are few. Particularly

as a child was later to serve him well as a scholar and pastor. He enrolled in the German Reformed Church's Classical School, soon to become Marshall College, where he was particularly impressed by the teaching and scholarship of F. A. Rauch. Upon graduation from Marshall College in 1838, Gerhart enrolled in the Seminary at Mercersburg, where he continued his studies with Rauch and also enjoyed the teaching of the new professor, John Nevin, who arrived in 1840.

Gerhart married Eliza Rickenbaugh in 1843—the fact that the wedding was officiated by John Nevin suggests that the relationship between Gerhart and Nevin was close; it was also complicated, as we shall see. After serving two pastorates in Pennsylvania, Gerhart spent two years as a missionary to the German immigrant community in Cincinnati, Ohio. His contacts in the Ohio Synod then led to a call in 1851 as President and Professor of Theology at the newly established Heidelberg College and Theological Seminary in Tiffin, Ohio, where he remained until 1855.

Like his teacher Nevin, Gerhart was administratively gifted, and with Nevin's retirement as President of Marshall College and the merger of that institution with Franklin College in Lancaster, Pennsylvania, Gerhart was called as President of the combined Franklin and Marshall College in 1855. During this period Gerhart also served as an editor and frequent contributor to the *Mercersburg Review*, and he was a member, along with Nevin and Schaff, of the committee that produced a new liturgy for the church.

In 1866 Gerhart was replaced by his former teacher John Nevin as President of Franklin and Marshall College, and in 1868 he was called back to Mercersburg as Professor of Didactic and Practical Theology at the Seminary.

helpful and accessible is Yrigoyen, "Emanuel V. Gerhart: Apologist," 485–500, upon which this summary is largely based.

Gerhart returned to Lancaster in 1871 with the transfer of the Seminary from Mercersburg to that city, and he served the Seminary until his death on May 6, 1904. The circumstances that led to his death are ironically symbolic of his lifetime of work in theological education. Descending the steep steps in front of the Seminary building while carrying a load of books, the eighty-six-year-old Gerhart fell and eventually succumbed to his injuries.

Gerhart's attitude toward the Mercersburg Theology of Nevin and Schaff has been the subject of some debate. During the early 1850s Gerhart expressed significant concerns and reservations about the direction of the Seminary at Mercersburg. On the basis of a detailed study of Gerhart's correspondence, Charles Yrigoyen has demonstrated that, while Gerhart affirmed the incarnational and sacramental orientation of the Mercersburg Theology, he grew increasingly disturbed by Nevin's hard-edged polemical style, his dalliance with Rome, and the positive appraisal of Roman Catholicism by both Nevin and Schaff.[20] Once Nevin left the Seminary and decided to remain within the German Reformed fold, it appears that Gerhart's concerns about the seminary subsided.

Gerhart was a productive scholar adept in historical and philosophical studies as well as theology; but his continuing legacy rests in large measure on his *Institutes of the Christian Religion* (1891, 1894), the only comprehensive systematic presentation of an incarnational theology in the Mercersburg tradition.[21] A number of characteristics

20. See the nuanced discussion in ibid., 494–97.

21. After many decades of neglect, Gerhart's theology began to receive scholarly attention beginning in the 1970s. See, e.g., Yrigoyen, "Emanuel V. Gerhart and the Mercersburg Theology"; Muller, "Emanuel V. Gerhart and the 'Christ-Idea' as Fundamental Principle"; Aubert, *German Roots of Nineteenth-Century American Theology*, 97–154.

of Gerhart's *Institutes* require mention, and in all of them Gerhart was standing in remarkable continuity with the Mercersburg Theology of Rauch, Nevin, and Schaff. First, this is self-consciously an exercise in *Reformed* dogmatics. Though John Calvin is modestly cited, the fact that Gerhart's work shares its title with Calvin's *magnum opus* is scarcely an accident.

Second, in contrast to the static truth claims of Catholic and Protestant Orthodoxy, Gerhart insisted on the principle of doctrinal development. He wrote: "The science of dogmatics pre-supposes the manifold growth of Christian life, and the development of doctrinal thought in the history of the Church during the past eighteen centuries."[22]

Third, Gerhart affirmed the central principle of Christian theology as the person of Christ, the God-Man. All the doctrines of Christianity must be viewed in relation to Christ as creator, revealer, sustainer, and savior. The first volume was introduced by Philip Schaff, who effusively endorsed Gerhart's Christocentric method with these words: "The divine-human person of Christ is the sum and substance of Christianity. This is the article of the standing or falling Church. All other doctrines that have been made fundamental and central, derive their significance from their connection with it."[23] In keeping with this, Gerhart opposed all other proposed central or foundational principles, whether divine sovereignty and predestination, the authority of Scripture, the doctrine of justification by faith, or the theme of covenant as it was expressed in the federal theology of the scholastic Reformed tradition.

Finally, in a methodological move that distinguishes Gerhart's systematic theology from other American Reformed efforts of his day, Gerhart markedly emphasized

22. Gerhart, *Institutes*, I:4. See Aubert, *German Roots*, 113–16.

23. Schaff, "Introduction," in Gerhart, *Institutes*, I:xii.

Christian consciousness, that is, the experience of the Christian. In his discussion of sources of theology, Gerhart distinguishes between the "objective source" and the "source in Christian consciousness." The objective source is none other than Jesus Christ himself as witnessed to in Scripture. Scripture, or the written word, is subordinate to the Word incarnate and must not be abstracted from Christ. But this objective source must become subjective in Christian consciousness through mystical union with Christ by faith and the Holy Spirit.[24] Gerhart writes: "Christ glorified is the one primordial and unchangeable source of divine knowledge. The source He is to His people not by the exertion of external influence, nor merely by verbal teaching, but by mystical union with them; a union begotten by the Holy Spirit and made effectual by personal faith. The transcendent Christ becomes an immanent vital principle, from which is developed a Christian ethical life and a Christian consciousness."[25] The roots of this emphasis on Christian consciousness rather clearly lie in German idealism (with its conviction that ultimate reality is ideal and thus involves consciousness) as well as the tradition of Schleiermacher (with its concern for "God consciousness") as it was conveyed to Mercersburg by the mediating theologians. With this focus on experience or Christian consciousness Gerhart sought to transcend the empiricist rationalism and Biblicism present in American Reformed Christianity generally (and especially at Old Princeton). Scripture is important, indeed essential, for Gerhart, but it must not be abstracted from Christ himself.

In the following chapters we will explore the contours of the Mercersburg Theology, and the order of treatment

24. See Gerhart, *Institutes*, I:33–78; Aubert, *German Roots*, 107–11.

25. Gerhart, *Institutes*, I:48.

is not accidental. We will examine the influences and contexts—both positive and negative—that contributed to this distinctive school. We will look at the initial polemical thrust by Nevin against American revivalism as involving a mistaken understanding of salvation. We will engage the Mercersburg alternative view of Christ and salvation. In order to explain where and how this salvation takes place, we will look at the Mercersburg view of history and the church. And finally, we will explore the life of the church in its ministry, worship, and liturgy.

QUESTIONS

1. How are the personal backgrounds of the Mercersburg protagonists reflected in their work?

2. In what ways did their respective personalities shape the careers of Nevin and Schaff?

3. How did E. V. Gerhart build upon the Mercersburg legacy of his teachers?

2

A TALE OF TWO CONTINENTS

THE MERCERSBURG THEOLOGY CAN be seen as a product of the encounter of two religious cultures—American and German. But it should not be viewed as simply an effort to replace American perspectives with German. Rather, the Mercersburg theologians brought German tools of historical analysis and theological method to bear on distinctly American problems, and the resulting synthesis continues to intrigue.

AMERICA

The nineteenth-century American context may be described broadly in terms of intellectual, social, and religious factors. The first is best engaged by an examination of the dominant philosophical system of the early national period—Scottish

Common Sense Realism—and here a bit of intellectual history is helpful. The roots of this school of thought lie in the broader movement we call British Empiricism and figures such as John Locke and David Hume. These were convinced that the path to truth is through sense experience (in contrast to the emphasis on pure reason in Continental philosophers such as Descartes, Leibniz, Spinoza, and their successors). David Hume's efforts to formulate a rigorously consistent empiricism, however, led to problems. He contended that all ideas in the mind consist of discrete sensory perceptions, but his consistent empiricism, with its focus on particularity, gave him no way to synthesize this flood of sensory data into a coherent and unified picture of reality. In the absence of such a synthesis, the reliability of knowledge, cause and effect, and even the notion of the mind itself were called into question.[1]

Scottish philosopher Thomas Reid (1710–1796) sought to answer Hume's skepticism in two ways: by reinforcing the connection between thought and reality and by providing a means of synthesizing sensory data into a coherent view of the world. Reid contended that Locke and his successors viewed ideas as mental objects that *represent* reality to the mind, and that this inevitably raised the question of whether such representation was accurate. Instead, Reid argued that ideas should be viewed, not as mental objects, but as mental acts of perception in which reality is directly apprehended. Reid also sought to explain what he took to be the axiomatic first principles essential to rational thought, such as the existence of material objects, cause and effect, the existence of the knowing self, and so forth. These, he argued, were a matter of the "common sense" possessed

1. On Hume, see Smith, *Philosophy of David Hume*; Mossner, *Life of David Hume*.

by all and were essential to the synthesis of sensory data by the mind.[2]

Certain characteristics of this philosophy of common sense must be noted. It was reflexively dualistic—the mind/matter distinction foundational to this empiricism was accompanied by other crucial distinctions such as subject and object, body and soul, nature and supernature, and so forth. And with this dualism went an emphasis on static particularity and induction from discrete facts. According to Dwight Bozeman, rather than reasoning deductively from the general to the particular, Reid and his successors preferred to generalize from the observation of particular phenomena, and the term "Baconian" became the popular descriptor of how disciplined inquiry should function.[3] All this involved, as Bozeman rightly observes, "a radically nominalist vision" of reality,[4] and this, as we shall see, stands in marked contrast to Mercersburg.

This philosophical system was introduced to America by John Witherspoon, who arrived from Scotland in 1768 to serve as President of the College of New Jersey, and soon it was adopted by much of the intellectual elite in America. As Sydney Ahlstrom has noted, this way of thinking was

2. See Grave, *Scottish Philosophy of Common Sense*; Holifield, *Gentlemen Theologians*, 110–26; Ahlstrom, "Scottish Philosophy and American Theology."

3. On this, see Bozeman, *Protestants in an Age of Science*.

4. Bozeman, *Protestants in an Age of Science*, 57. Nominalism was a late medieval development, associated with figures such as William of Occam, that denied the real existence of universals (e.g., humankind) and asserted that only particulars exist. Universals are viewed as only names or terms that we apply to individual existents. It was also strongly voluntaristic, holding that the world is best understood as the product of the divine will rather than divine reason. With this voluntarism came a corresponding pessimism about the capacity of human reason. Mercersburg opposed both these aspects.

extraordinarily useful in the early nineteenth-century context for addressing the issues of the day:

> The Scottish Philosophy was an apologetical philosophy, *par excellence*. And the secret of its success, I think, lay in its dualism, epistemological, ontological, and cosmological. Its other advantages were auxiliary. Reid's theory affirmed a clean subject-object distinction. The world which men perceived was in no sense constituted by consciousness. On the mind-matter problem dualism facilitated an all-out attack on both materialism and idealism, as well as the pantheism that either type of monistic analysis could lead to. Furthermore, by a firm separation of the Creator and His creation, the Scottish thinkers preserved the orthodox notion of God's transcendence, and made revelation necessary . . . The Scottish philosophy, in short, was a winning combination.[5]

The sociology of the early national period also requires mention. The possibilities of the New World facilitated the rise of utilitarian individualism—the power of the industrious individual to achieve success without regard for hereditary social station, and the American Revolution unleashed powerful impulses for freedom and popular sovereignty that had remarkable implications for traditional social structures and authorities. As Nathan Hatch rightly observes, "the Revolution dramatically expanded the circle of people who considered themselves capable of thinking for themselves about issues of freedom, equality, sovereignty, and representation. Respect for authority, tradition,

5. Ahlstrom, "Scottish Philosophy and American Theology," 267–68.

station, and education eroded."[6] Crucial for our purposes is the combining of the political and the religious in this early national context. Once again, Hatch writes that "many humble Christians in America began to redeem a dual legacy. They yoked strenuous demands for revivals, in the name of George Whitefield, with calls for the expansion of popular sovereignty, in the name of the Revolution. Linking these equally potent traditions sent American Christianity cascading in many creative directions in the early republic. Church authorities had few resources to restrain this surge of movements fueled by the passions of ordinary people."[7]

The populist, experientialist, and individualistic sort of Christianity that emerged from this remarkable period of intellectual ferment and social change provided the foil for the Mercersburg Theology. The revivalism that emerged during the first Great Awakening (1739–1742) under the leadership of George Whitefield, Jonathan Edwards, Gilbert Tennant, and others was an appeal to the individual, sometimes over against established church authority, to embrace the experience of personal conversion, and this conversion experience was conceived as an immediate and emotionally charged experience of divine grace.

With this came more radical versions of the traditional Protestant notions of private judgment and the priesthood of all believers. The Reformers had stressed the competence of Christians to read Scripture for themselves without the guidance of the magisterium, or teaching office, of the Catholic church, but they never dreamed that biblical interpretation should ignore the collective wisdom of the church. But in early nineteenth-century America private judgment for many came to mean not only that anyone can read the Bible for themselves but also that education

6. Hatch, *Democratization of American Christianity*, 6.

7. Ibid., 7.

and the wisdom of the church are unnecessary and perhaps even impediments. Likewise the priesthood of all believers, deployed by the Reformers to oppose Catholic notions of a special priesthood empowered to perform the miracle of transubstantiation in the Mass, came to mean that Christians approach God directly without the mediation or help of the church's means of grace.

Not surprisingly, this religious individualism resulted in sectarianism as American Protestantism in the early national period exploded into a wide variety of sects and groups. Ironically, these groups, which ostensibly championed the "common man," were often led by strong, domineering figures, such that traditional authority of church and creed was often replaced by the personal authority of leaders. Nathan Hatch writes, "Attempting to erase the difference between leaders and followers, American opened the door to religious demagogues. Despite popular acclaim, these leaders could exercise tyranny unimagined by elites in the more controlled environment of the colonial era."[8]

Certain themes predominate amidst these developments. The sovereignty of the individual in matters of salvation and religious judgment accelerated the eclipse of Calvinism in the American context. The suspicion directed against elites and their institutions placed an ever greater emphasis on religious immediacy, the capacity of the individual Christian to encounter God directly. And finally, we find a persistent rationalism at work in which the "common sense" of the "common man" was exalted at the expense of mystery and tradition. What emerged, in short, was a populist theological hermeneutic.

The sacraments are an interesting test case in for this rational immediatism. Traditional notions of sacramental efficacy, whether spiritual incorporation into the church by

8. Ibid., 16.

baptism or the presence of Christ in the Lord's Supper, were mysterious and resistant to rational explanation. Furthermore, the traditional sacramentalism of the church implied that divine grace is mediated to the individual by the church and therefore that the church is in some sense prior to the individual—something that the prevailing sectarian individualistic immediatism could not allow. Thus American views on the sacraments became increasingly baptistic and memorialist—baptism was seen by many as a sign of one's faith and conversion, and the Lord's Supper was nothing more than a mental exercise remembering Christ's work on the cross. In short, the religious center of gravity was shifting decisively from the congregation or group to the individual.

GERMANY

The influence of Germany upon nineteenth-century theology cannot be understood apart from the political and cultural developments of the period. Long a region of duchies, kingdoms, and principalities loosely confederated in the Holy Roman Empire, by the early nineteenth century Germany was achieving political unification under the auspices of the Prussian state. One of the instruments of this political unification was the Prussian Union Church, which combined the German Lutherans and Reformed into a single state church. Further evidence of national vigor was the founding of the University of Berlin in 1810, which became the academic home for philosophers such as Hegel, Fichte, and Schelling, as well as the great theologian Friedrich Schleiermacher.

Three intellectual developments in Germany are of particular importance for understanding the Mercersburg Theology. The first is the idealist ontology and epistemology which developed in response to the seminal work of the philosopher Immanuel Kant. Kant had responded to the skepticism of David Hume by emphasizing the activity of the mind in ordering sensory data. But if a good deal of what we know is contributed by the mind itself, this issues in an epistemological skepticism of another sort: what guarantee is there that appearances correspond to reality? Kant famously argued that pure reason can know things as they appear to us (phenomena) but not things in themselves (noumena), and thus there are rather severe limitations on pure reason.

But some influential thinkers were unwilling to accept Kant's noumenal/phenomenal dualism. If reality itself is ultimately rational thought (ontological idealism), then true knowledge of ultimate reality is possible after all. Thus G. W. F. Hegel argued that finite reason is Absolute Mind or Spirit coming to self-consciousness, and that all world process—nature, history, finite thought—is the dialectical unfolding of Absolute Spirit.[9]

Closely related to this ontological idealism were organic, developmental views of history. If history is the unfolding of the Absolute, as Hegel contended, then reality is developmental rather than static, and Hegel's contemporary Schelling further emphasized the organic character of this process as the life of God unfolds in history in a dialectic of being and becoming. Needless to say, this was intoxicating stuff! Worth noting is the way this view of history as the organic unfolding of the divine life involves an identification of divine becoming and historical process such that history is ultimate reality, and the intense interest during the nineteenth century in historical studies in general and church history in particular makes sense in light of this.

9. See Hodgson, "Georg Wilhelm Friedrich Hegel."

Third, we see the rise of Christocentric approaches to theology in which the Incarnation becomes the central organizing principle. The key figure here is the theologian Friedrich D. E. Schleiermacher, who taught at the University of Berlin and preached regularly at the *Dreifaltigkeitskirche* (Trinity Church) there. While Kant had viewed the figure of Jesus as little more than a helpful teacher and example of moral truth (with the content of that moral truth also available to practical reason), Schleiermacher inaugurated a new era in theology in which Jesus was viewed as both central and necessary. Schleiermacher believed that religion is grounded in something more fundamental than either reason or ethics—in a particular sort of pre-theoretical experience of God that Schleiermacher describes as a feeling of absolute or utter dependence upon God.[10] He also presented the figure of Jesus as the archetypal ideal of humanity realized in history, and what distinguishes Jesus from other human beings is the "constant potency of his God-consciousness" and his "unclouded blessedness" or sinlessness. Although Schleiermacher rejected the church's creedal Christological doctrine of two natures in hypostatic union, he nevertheless described this profound experience of God as a "veritable existence of God in him."[11]

For Schleiermacher, Christ is the "Second Adam," the one in whom humanity is redeemed and raised to a new level of existence. Christians are incorporated into this new reality as they are assumed "into the power of his God-consciousness" and "into the fellowship of his unclouded blessedness."[12] The centrality of Christ for Schleiermacher is evident in his definition of Christianity as "a monotheistic faith belonging to the teleological type of religion,

10. Schleiermacher, *Christian Faith*, 12.

11. Ibid., 377–89.

12. Ibid., 425, 431.

and is essentially distinguished from other such faiths by the fact that everything in it is related to the redemption accomplished by Jesus of Nazareth."[13] Schleiermacher's christocentrism and his focus on consciousness were extraordinarily influential on the Mercersburg theologians, and John Nevin referred to him as "the theological Origen of his age."[14]

Particularly important for Mercersburg was a group of German theologians of the generation after Hegel and Schleiermacher—among them the historian August Neander, and theologians such as Julius Müller, I. A. Dorner, and Carl Ullmann—who sought to mediate between the more daring approaches of Hegel and Schleiermacher on the one hand and orthodoxy on the other. In general, the tendency of these "Mediating Theologians" was to appropriate broader insights of Hegel and Schleiermacher (e.g., Hegel's developmental view of history and Schleiermacher's christocentrism) while moving back in the direction of orthodox Christianity. For example, the speculative panentheism of Hegel was viewed with suspicion, and Schleiermacher's approach of grounding theology in the "feeling of utter dependence" was seen as too subjective. The Mediating Theologians also moved back in the direction of Chalcedonian Christology, though they framed the relationship of the divine and human natures in Christ in more dynamic terms. Finally, they criticized Hegel and Schleiermacher for inadequate understandings of sin and the estrangement between God and humanity.[15] We may say that the Mercers-

13. Ibid., 52.

14. Nevin, "Liebner's Christology," 59 (MTSS IV, 95). Origen of Alexandria was a third-century church father whose massive influence is seen in many subsequent debates and doctrinal developments.

15. For a brief example of the Mediating Theology, see Ullmann, "Das Wesen des Christentums," loosely translated by Nevin as

burg Theology was a recasting of the German mediating theology in a form that addressed the American situation.

TENSION POINTS

It is useful to recognize the salient differences between the American and German contexts. Philosophically, the Scottish Common Sense philosophy ascendant in America during this period was fundamentally disjunctive and dualistic. It was concerned with the many, with finite particularity rather than integration and ultimate unity. By contrast, the German idealist philosophy was fundamentally integrative and anti-dualistic. It was concerned with the unity that transcends the experience of diversity.

Moreover, the German organic and developmental approach to history stood in marked contrast to the static and essentially ahistorical sensibility of many Americans during this period, for whom history was just a collection of facts from which one could pick and choose. As we noted earlier, many Americans found it quite plausible to say that the "true church" faded out of existence after the death of the apostles, only to be rediscovered by Martin Luther and the Protestant Reformation. The Mercersburg theologians insisted, however, that the Reformation did not emerge *de novo*, that Luther and Calvin built on the foundation of the early and medieval church, and that there is an organic and developmental relationship between the various epochs of church history.

These German preferences for unity and development help to explain the distinctiveness of Mercersburg over against the prevailing American Protestantism of the day. The religious individualism of American Protestantism and the corporate ecclesial sensibility of Mercersburg were like

---

"Preliminary Essay," in *Mystical Presence*, 13–47 (MTSS I, 15–39).

oil and water. For most Americans, the individual was sovereign—in matters political and religious. The revivalism of the nineteenth century was designed expressly to appeal to the decision of this sovereign individual and the sectarianism of a plethora of religious groups and denominations was the inevitable result. For Mercersburg, however, individual Christians find their identity by being incorporated into something greater than themselves—the church, where they are nourished and sustained by the means of grace.

Related to this is the dramatic difference in religious sensibility between a theology of immediatism and a theology of mediation. For many American Protestants, the sovereign individual encounters the grace of God directly and without the mediation of church and sacraments. To be sure, the Christian's immediate relationship with God is made possible by the work of Christ, but the earlier Catholic and Reformational notion that all the blessings of salvation are received through the believer's union with Christ, and that this Christ is received through the sacraments of the church is rather foreign to this way of thinking. For Mercersburg, however, Jesus Christ is the great mediator and the church as the body of Christ is the means whereby divine grace is bestowed.

QUESTIONS

1. In what ways did the philosophical traditions of British empiricism and German idealism stand in conflict?

2. What were the cultural roots of American individualism?

3. How did revivalism impact nineteenth-century American religion?

4. What factors and influences help to account for the powerful interest in the figure of Jesus Christ as central for theology?

3

REVIVALISM ENGAGED

THE FIRST ARTICULATION OF the Mercersburg Theology came in the context of debate over revivalism and its impact on the German churches of Pennsylvania. John Nevin is the primary figure in this chapter, and his most significant contribution to this issue predated Schaff's arrival. In order better to understand this we need to examine the history of revivalism in America and the conversionist model of piety that accompanied it. Certainly no single influence has done more to shape the piety, practice, and theology of American Protestant Christianity, and so it is important to know something of how American Protestants got from the early Puritans in the seventeenth century to Billy Graham in the twentieth.

REVIVALISM IN AMERICA

The roots of American revivalism lie in the Puritan concern for heart religion and true conversion. The Puritans came to America determined to purify the theology, the practices, and the membership of the church, and to ensure that the church was made up of those who truly knew Christ. With the freedom to put their program into practice in New England, Puritans quickly moved to require a convincing "relation" or narrative of one's conversion to Christ. This represented a change from previous Protestant practice, which simply required a profession of faith and good behavior. The substance of these "relations" drew heavily on descriptions of the morphology of conversion found in the writings of English Puritan theologians such as Richard Sibbes and William Perkins. Perkins, for example, identified ten stages of evangelical conversion, including knowledge of God's law, a sense of sin and the hopelessness of achieving salvation by one's own effort, coming to faith, the beginnings of assurance, and gradual transformation of life.[1] The Puritans, of course, were Calvinists, and they regarded this process as the outworking of the sovereignty of God who chooses the elect for salvation. But two additional points must also be noted here—the introspective subjectivity of this process and the fact that it often took considerable time.

The First Great Awakening in the 1740s marks the next stage in the development of American revivalism. This remarkable event swept the colonies in short order from South Carolina to Massachusetts. American Congregational and Presbyterian ministers such as Jonathan Edwards and Gilbert Tennant played significant roles, but

1. See Morgan, *Visible Saints*, 68. See also Caldwell, *The Puritan Conversion Narrative*.

the most prominent figure was the "Grand Itinerant"—the evangelical Anglican George Whitefield (1714–1770), whose preaching attracted large crowds. Here we see several developments. A new style of preaching emerged, involving evocative sermons designed to elicit conversion. The process of conversion was streamlined as listeners were exhorted to experience the "new birth" there and then, rather than waiting for the older and lengthy Puritan morphology of conversion to run its course. Whitefield also effectively wrote the job description for a new and lasting figure in American religion—the itinerant or traveling evangelist whose ministry was tied to no particular parish or congregation.

There was something both old and new about the First Great Awakening. Like their Puritan forbears, Edwards, Tennant, and Whitefield were still Calvinists. They regarded the revivals of their day as a supernatural work of the Spirit of God who brings the elect to salvation. But the Puritan emphasis on introspective subjectivity was, if anything, heightened during this period. Whitefield, for example, insisted that the "new birth" was an experience so immediate, intense, and palpable that one could not fail to recognize it when it happened.[2] In retrospect, it is clear that these two emphases—a theocentric stress on divine sovereignty and an increasingly anthropocentric focus on human experience and agency—would eventually come to stand in tension with each other.

The Second Great Awakening was the third stage in the development of American revivalism. We apply the term Second Great Awakening to the revivals that began in New England in the 1790s, to the frontier camp meetings in Kentucky and Tennessee, such as Cane Ridge, in the

2. See Heimert and Miller, "Introduction," in *The Great Awakening*, xxviii.

first decade of the nineteenth century, and to the revivals in upstate New York during the 1820s and 1830s that were particularly associated with Charles Grandison Finney (1792–1875). Without Finney in particular, American religion would look quite different today.

As we noted above, the leaders of the First Great Awakening were Calvinists who believed that revivals were a miraculous work of the Spirit of God. Finney, however, was part of a broader trend during this period away from Calvinism and toward an emphasis on human freedom and agency. Americans increasingly believed that human beings are sovereign in both politics and religion. Consistent with this, Finney contended that there is nothing miraculous about conversion and revival. Rather, they are simply the result of the application of appropriate techniques. In his *Lectures on Revivals of Religion* Finney wrote: "It is not a miracle, or dependent on a miracle, in any sense. It is a purely philosophical [i.e., natural] result of the right use of the constituted means." Finney went on to compare revivals to a farmer sowing seed and expecting a harvest: "In the Bible, the word of God is compared to grain, and preaching is compared to sowing seed, and the results to the springing up and growth of the crop. And the result is just as philosophical in the one case, as in the other, and is as naturally connected with the cause."[3]

In line with this conviction, Finney emphasized a variety of techniques, or "New Measures," designed to elicit conversions: direct and accessible preaching, prayers for people by name and emotional public prayers by women, house-to-house canvassing of cities and towns, and, perhaps most famously, the use of the "anxious bench"—a bench or row of pews at the front of the church to which the unconverted were urged to come and contemplate their

3. Finney, *Lectures on Revivals of Religion*, 12–13.

sins under the direct gaze of the evangelist. Rather clearly, the intent was to manipulate the emotions so as to induce a conversion experience. While certainly the most famous revivalist of his day, Finney was not the only one promoting such techniques. Itinerant Methodist ministers had long been preaching in similar fashion, and Finney himself spawned a host of imitators who traversed the "northwest frontier" region of upstate New York—a region that came to be known as the "burned-over district" because of the way this intense, methodological revivalism repeatedly swept through, leaving the populace emotionally exhausted and the area spiritually barren.[4]

Efforts were also made to develop a theology consistent with these revivalist practices. Not surprisingly, such efforts often focused especially on questions of human agency and ability, and traditional Calvinist notions of total depravity and helplessness in the face of sin were downplayed. A key figure in this process was the New England Calvinist theologian Nathaniel William Taylor (1786–1858), who taught at Yale Divinity School from 1822 to 1857. In an important 1828 sermon, Taylor contended that depravity does not consist in a sinful human nature inherited from Adam, or in any disposition or tendency to sin. Rather, human sinfulness consists simply in the act of sinning, and depravity in the fact that "such is their nature, that they will sin and only sin in all appropriate circumstances of their being."[5] In other words, sin cannot be explained by any antecedent causes, and, while inevitable, sin is not necessary. Furthermore, while all human beings sin, and sin is universal to humanity, human beings have the power to do otherwise. In these ways, Taylor softened traditional Reformed teachings on human depravity and laid a foundation for revival-

4. See Cross, *Burned-Over District.*

5. Taylor, "Concio ad Clerum," 222.

ist techniques that presupposed a more optimistic view of human nature. From the perspective of such "Taylorism," revivals were not so much a work of God as the work of preachers who moved people to repentance and faith.

By the time Nevin arrived in Mercersburg in 1840, methodological revivalism in the style of Finney was already a matter of controversy among the German Reformed and Lutheran churches in Pennsylvania.[6] When a visiting minister tried to implement Finneyite practices at the German Reformed Church in Mercersburg, Nevin took a stand against the practices, and in 1843 the first edition of his *The Anxious Bench* was published. This critique of revivalist practice elicited considerable controversy, and the next year a revised and expanded edition appeared in which Nevin responded to his critics. This second edition was simultaneously a rather subtle phenomenological study of the psychology of popular revivalism, an analysis of the theological presuppositions informing revivalism, and the first cogent presentation of the Mercersburg Theology.

THE ANXIOUS BENCH

Nevin's deep interest in his new communion is immediately evident in his Preface to the second edition, where he repeatedly underscored his concern for the "old German Churches" of Pennsylvania and banged the drum of denominational identity. The anxious bench, he declared, has its origins in a source alien to both the Reformed and Lutheran traditions: "The system in question is in its principle and soul neither Calvinism nor Lutheranism, but Wesleyan *Methodism*. Those who are urging it upon the old German Churches, are in fact doing as much as they can to turn them over into the arms of Methodism . . . Already the life

6. See Yoder, "Bench versus the Catechism," 14–23.

of Methodism, in this country, is actively at work among other sects, which owe no fellowship with it in form."[7] This dismissive reference to Methodism raises certain questions, for later in the work Nevin will condemn the anxious bench as Finneyite and as "Taylorism," influences that have more to do with the conversionist piety of New England Calvinism than with the Wesleys.[8]

In the first chapter Nevin indicates that his concern is not for the anxious bench itself; rather, the practice is a symbol or trope for a system of religion that comes to expression in New Measures revivalism. He does not mince words as his objections to the anxious bench are developed over the course of the first six chapters of the book. The anxious bench, he says, is a novelty; it is not compatible with the historic practices of the church. All pragmatic arguments from the popularity and apparent efficacy of New Measures are rejected, and Nevin insists that the anxious bench is a form of "quackery" that substitutes transient psychological manipulation for real and lasting spiritual power. As Nevin puts it, "Conversion is everything, sanctification nothing. Religion is not regarded as the life of God in the soul that must be cultivated in order that it may grow, but rather as a transient excitement to be renewed from time to time by suitable stimulants presented to the imagination."[9]

In his polemic we also sense an elitism at work, and it is rather clear that some of Nevin's distaste for the New Measures stemmed from the fact that he regarded them as tacky and embarrassing. "As the spirit of the anxious bench," he opined, "tends to disorder, so it connects itself also naturally and readily with a certain vulgarism of feeling in religion

7. Nevin, *Anxious Bench*, vii (*Catholic and Reformed*, 12–13).

8. Nevin's complaints with Methodism are explored in Yrigoyen, "Mercersburg's Quarrel with Methodism," 194–203.

9. Nevin, *Anxious Bench*, 63–64 (*Catholic and Reformed*, 57).

that is always injurious to the worship of God, and often shows itself absolutely irreverent and profane."[10] And echoing a common theme in the anti-revivalist literature of the day, Nevin viewed the expanded role of women in revivalist circles as further evidence of "grossness and coarseness in religion." He wrote: "One striking illustration of the coarseness of this spirit is found in the disposition it has shown in all ages to set aside the rule which forbids women to speak publicly in religious assemblies. Nature itself may be said to teach us that woman cannot quit her sphere of relative subordination with regard to man without dishonoring herself and losing her proper strength."[11]

More substantial is Nevin's psychological and theological analysis of the phenomenon of revivalism. The bench, he argues, poses a false issue for the conscience in that it substitutes the outward act of going forward to the anxious bench for an actual encounter with God, and it creates a host of distractions in the minds of those who are genuinely concerned about their spiritual state.[12] But perhaps most important, the anxious bench is, according to Nevin, a "heresy." The root problem here is an overestimation of human ability and an underestimation of the problem of sin: "Finneyism is only Taylorism reduced to practice, the speculative heresy of New-Haven actualized in common life. A low, shallow, pelagianizing theory of religion runs through it from beginning to end."[13] In this context Nevin

10. Ibid., 107 (*Catholic and Reformed*, 89).

11. Ibid., 111 (*Catholic and Reformed*, 95).

12. Ibid., 65–84 (*Catholic and Reformed*, 59–74).

13. Ibid., 114 (*Catholic and Reformed*, 98). Pelagius was an early fifth-century heretic who emphasized free will and held that original sin is nothing more than the bad example of the first parents passed down from generation to generation. He was opposed by Augustine and others.

references the portion of upstate New York in which the revivalist efforts of Finney and others had been concentrated,
and the sad results for religion in those areas.

> The proper fruits of Pelagianism follow the
> system invariably in proportion exactly to the
> extent in which it may be suffered in any case
> to prevail. A most ample field for instruction
> with regard to this point, for all who care to
> receive instruction, is presented in the history
> of the great religious movement over which Mr.
> Finney presided some years ago in certain parts
> of this country. Years of faithful pastoral service
> on the part of a different order of ministers
> working in a wholly different style have hardly
> yet sufficed in the northern section of the state
> of New York to restore to something like spiri-
> tual fruitfulness and beauty the field over which
> this system then passed as a wasting fire in the
> fullness of its strength.[14]

In the final chapter Nevin presents his comprehensive
alternative to the "system of the anxious bench"—what he
terms the "system of the catechism." Just as the anxious
bench in this work was an exercise in theological synec-
doche—a symbol for the larger system of New-Measures
conversionism—so also the catechism stands as symbol
for the system of Christian nurture involving catechetical
instruction, pastoral care, and the ministry of the word and
sacrament, in short, the traditional means of grace found in
the bosom of the church.

Immediately Nevin hones in on what he regards as the
Achilles heel of the anxious bench—an abstract individualism in which the convert is treated as a volitional agent

14. Ibid., 116–17 (*Catholic and Reformed*, 99). See also Cross,
Burned-Over District.

apart from the concrete situation in which he or she exists. For example, the problem of sin is not simply in the act of sinning (as Nathaniel William Taylor had maintained) but rather in a sinful condition, an organic disease, that all human beings share with Adam. Thus the general must precede the individual. Nevin goes on to argue that the "generic life," the organic state of being "in Adam," must be countered by a union with Christ that is just as deep and organic.

> Man is the subject of it [i.e., salvation], but not the author of it in any sense. His nature is restorable, but it can never restore itself. The restoration to be real, must begin *beyond* the individual. In this case as in the other the general must go before the particular, and support it as its proper ground. Thus humanity fallen in Adam, is made to undergo a resurrection in Christ, and so restored flows over organically as in the other case to all in whom its life appears. The sinner is saved then by an inward living union with Christ as real as the bond by which he has been joined in the first instance to Adam.[15]

The source of this saving restoration, Christ himself, is to be found in the life and ministry of the church. Here once again the general precedes the individual. The church is not to be thought of as merely the aggregate of individual Christians, as a "sandheap" of individuals as Nevin often terms it. Rather, the church is the source of the organic saving life of Christ.

> This spiritual constitution is brought to bear upon him in the Church by means of institutions and agencies which God has appointed, and clothed with power expressly for this end. Hence

15. Ibid., 125 (*Catholic and Reformed*, 107).

> where the system of the Catechism prevails great
> account is made of the Church, and all reliance
> placed upon the means of grace comprehended
> in its constitution as all-sufficient under God for
> the accomplishment of its own purposes . . . Due
> regard is had to the idea of the Church as some-
> thing more than a bare abstraction, the con-
> ception of an aggregate of parts mechanically
> brought together. It is apprehended rather as an
> organic life springing perpetually from the same
> ground, and identical with itself at every point.
> In this view the Church is truly the mother of all
> her children. They do not impart life to her, but
> she imparts life to them. Here again the general
> is left to go before the particular, and to condi-
> tion all its manifestations.[16]

Nevin then explores the implications of this churchly sensibility. Children are baptized into the church as infants, and the expectation should be that they will grow up into faith as they are nurtured by the means of grace, and this without need for the "sudden and violent" emotional parox-ysms of methodological revivalism: "it is counted not only possible, but altogether natural that children growing up in the bosom of the Church under the faithful application of the means of grace should be quickened into spiritual life in a comparatively quiet way . . . without being able at all to trace the process by which the glorious change has been effected."[17] In keeping with this, the family is seen as fun-damental to the life of the church and the spiritual nurture provided there essential.

In addition, the ministry of the word and sacrament is also central to this "system of the Catechism." This, for Nevin, includes not only the stated weekly services of the

16. Ibid., 129 (*Catholic and Reformed*, 110–11).

17. Ibid., 130 (*Catholic and Reformed*, 111).

congregation, but also household visitation by ministers. Here Nevin concedes that such careful and ongoing pastoral care may be less exciting than the sound and fury of the anxious bench, but he avers that "the common and the constant are of vastly more account than the special and transient."[18] Such was the system employed by the Reformers, Nevin argues, and he places special emphasis on the effectiveness of the lengthy pastoral ministry of the seventeenth-century English Puritan Richard Baxter at Kidderminster as described in Baxter's famous work *The Reformed Pastor*.

In this exposition of the "system of the catechism" we see, at least in outline, crucial themes that would be central to the Mercersburg Theology as it developed—organic union with Christ, the generic humanity of Adam and Christ that determine the identity of those joined with them, the mediation of the church, the priority of the general over the particular, and the church over the individual. In subsequent chapters we will see these themes developed.

QUESTIONS

1. In what ways was revivalism affecting the German Reformed Church in Nevin's time?

2. What are the key differences between the "system of the anxious bench" and the "system of the catechism"?

3. Why did Nevin regard the anxious bench as a "heresy"?

---

18. Ibid., 136 (*Catholic and Reformed*, 116).

4

CHRIST AND SALVATION

THE MERCERSBURG THEOLOGIANS RESOLUTELY affirmed
the centrality of Christ—as creator and redeemer—not
only for theology narrowly considered but for all reality
and human endeavor. John Nevin wrote in the first volume
of the *Mercersburg Review*: "The Incarnation is the deepest
and most comprehensive fact, in the economy of the world.
Jesus Christ authenticates himself, and all truth and reality
besides; or rather all truth and reality are such, only by the
relation in which they stand to him, as their great centre
and last ground."[1] Thus Christology assumes the status of
a "central dogma" for the movement; no aspect of theology was to be abstracted from Christ, and here Mercersburg was drawing on the influence of Schleiermacher and

---

1. Nevin, "The Apostles' Creed," 315. On this aspect of the Mercersburg Theology, see Muller, "Emanuel V. Gerhart on the 'Christ
Idea' as Fundamental Principle," 97–117.

the German Mediating Theologians. The distinctiveness of the Mercersburg Christology over against prevailing nineteenth-century American Protestant ways of thinking is evident in the way that certain key themes are developed.

CHRIST AS THE SECOND ADAM

Crucial here is the Mercersburg view of Christ as the "second Adam," the one in whom humanity is redeemed and elevated into union with God. Here there were rich antecedents in the Christian tradition upon which the Mercersburg theologians could draw. Significantly, the Apostle Paul had presented Christ as a "second Adam"; just as sin, disobedience, death, and condemnation came through Adam, so righteousness, obedience, life, and justification come through Christ (see Romans 5:12–21; 1 Corinthians 15:22, 42–50). This parallel between the two Adams was then developed at great length by the second-century church father Irenaeus of Lyon (c. 130–202) in his doctrine of "recapitulation" (from the Greek term *anakephalaiosis*, or "summing up under a new head"). Three themes in Irenaeus are of particular importance for our understanding of Mercersburg. First, there is the programmatic parallel between the two Adams—Irenaeus famously contended that Christ as the second Adam recapitulates the pattern of human existence, replacing Adam's disobedience with his own obedience and sanctifying the whole of human life.[2] Second, there is the solidarity of human beings in these two figures—humanity participates in Adam by natural generation and Christians participate in Christ through sacramental incorporation into the church as the mystical body of Christ. And third, there is the elevation of the church into union with God by the Incarnation and work of Christ, as human beings are

2. See especially Irenaeus, *Against Heresies* I:440–58.

sanctified in Christ. The pattern of thinking in Mercersburg is insistently Irenaean, and both Nevin and Schaff often referred to Irenaeus and recapitulation. As Nevin wrote: "Christ must be of the same length and breadth in all respects with humanity as a whole, in order to be at all a real and true Mediator. He must be commensurate with the universal process of humanity from infancy to old age, as well as with its mere numerical extent . . . He sanctified infancy and child-hood, says Irenaeus, by making them stages of his own life. This expresses a just and sound feeling."[3]

To this biblical and patristic foundation was added the influence of the German theologian Friedrich Schleier-macher and his Mediating Theology successors with their idealism. For Schleiermacher, Christ is the "second Adam," the archetypal ideal and culmination of human destiny: "As everything which has been brought into human life through Christ is presented as a new creation, so Christ Himself is the Second Adam, the beginner and originator of this more perfect human life, or the completion of the creation of man."[4] According to the speculative idealism of Hegel, another powerful influence on the Mediating Theologians, in Christ the idea of divine-human unity has been concretely realized, and these ways of thinking suggested that the Incarnation was not so much a contingent response to human sin as a metaphysical necessity. Nevin in particular wrestled with this question at length in extended reviews of notable German works.[5] While clearly sympathetic to the idealist formulation, Nevin did not pronounce decisively on the question. This issue is important for our understanding of the antecedents and character of the Mer-

3. Nevin, "Noel on Baptism," 249 (MTSS VI, 99–100).

4. Schleiermacher, *The Christian Faith*, 367.

5. See Nevin, "Liebner's Christology"; "*Cur Deus Homo*" (MTSS IV, 87–135).

cersburg movement, and we will return to this question later in this chapter.

With this Irenaean framework came an approach to the relationship between the person and work of Christ, and this in turn had profound implications for the Mercersburg understanding of the experience of salvation. The death of Christ was not merely an exercise of legal substitution in which Christ takes the place of the sinner and absorbs the punishment the sinner deserves, though that forensic dimension is not denied. Rather, the cross and resurrection of Christ were a mighty victory over sin, death, and the devil, the culmination of Christ's life of obedience in which the powers of darkness were progressively overcome. As Nevin put it in *The Mystical Presence*:

> The VALUE of Christ's sufferings and death, as well as of his entire life, in relation to men, springs wholly from the view of the incarnation now presented. The Assumption of humanity on the part of the Logos involved the necessity of suffering, as the only way in which the new life with which it was thus joined could triumph over the law of sin and death it was called to surmount. The passion of the Son of God was the world's spiritual crisis, in which the principle of health came to its last struggle with the principle of disease, and burst forth from the very bosom of the grace itself in the form of immortality. This was the atonement, Christ's victory over sin and hell. As such it forms the only medium of salvation to men.[6]

In the same context, Nevin makes clear that the imputation of the righteousness of Christ to the Christian

---

6. Nevin, *Mystical Presence*, 166 (MTSS I, 148). On this, see Nichols, *Romanticism in American Theology*, 144–46.

is not denied. Rather, Christ's substitutionary work only avails for salvation as the Christian is united with Christ by faith. Here's Nevin assumed a much closer relationship of the person and work of Christ than many of his American Protestant contemporaries in that the benefits of Christ's work cannot be abstracted from his person. The benefits of salvation are not received, Nevin insists, by some sort of external, quasi-commercial transaction: "Not by the atonement then, as something made over to us separately from Christ's person, are we placed in the possession of salvation and life; but only by the atonement as comprehended in his person itself, and received through faith in this form."[7] Thus a key concept for understanding this two-Adams construction is "participation"; sinful humanity participates in the First Adam, while redeemed humanity participates in the Second: "When Christ died and rose, humanity died and rose at the same time in his person; not figuratively, but truly; just as it had fallen before in the person of Adam."[8]

THE FALLEN HUMANITY OF CHRIST

The disease metaphor used above to describe Christ's work points to another important aspect of the Mercersburg Christology. Emphasizing the solidarity of Christ with those he came to save as well as the healing of fallen human nature and its elevation into union with God, the Mercersburg theologians frequently spoke of Christ's "fallen humanity." A broken and weakened humanity (i.e., humanity in its post-fall condition) was assumed by Christ in the Incarnation, and this brokenness has been healed in Christ. Nevin writes:

7. Nevin, *Mystical Presence*, 240 (MTSS I, 208).
8. Ibid., 166 (MTSS I, 148).

> In taking our nature upon him, he was made in all respects like as we are, only without sin. (Heb. iv. 15. v. 2, 7). he appeared 'in the likeness of sinful flesh' (Rom. viii.3); 'made of a woman, made under the law' (Gal. iv.4). The humanity which he assumed was fallen, subject to infirmity, and liable to death. In the end, 'he was crucified through weakness' (2 Cor. xiii.4). Under all this low estate however, the power of a divine life was always actively present, wrestling as it were with the law of death it was called to conquer, and sure of its proper victory at last. This victory was displayed in the resurrection.[9]

Such language, for Mercersburg, implied no compromise of the sinlessness of Christ. In fact, Philip Schaff in a number of contexts argued from the sinlessness of Christ's humanity to his divinity.[10] It does, however, underscore that the Mercersburg concerns were at least as much ontological as they were forensic. More than forgiveness is required; sinful and broken humanity must be healed and restored, and this restoration takes place in the person of Christ.

This view regarding the "sinful humanity" of Christ was unusual in its nineteenth-century context; it was particularly associated with the defrocked Scottish Presbyterian minister Edward Irving (1792–1834), who was a key influence on the founding of the Catholic Apostolic Church in London in the 1830s (the liturgy of which would later influence Mercersburg). But it found ardent champions in the twentieth-century theologies of Karl Barth and especially Thomas F. Torrance, who regarded the denial of it as "the Latin heresy" (i.e., a misunderstanding to which the

9. Ibid., 223 (MTSS I, 194).

10. See, e.g., Schaff, *Moral Character of Christ*.

Christian West with its forensic preoccupation was especially susceptible).[11]

THE GENERIC HUMANITY OF CHRIST

As we have seen, Mercersburg with its emphasis on the corporate stressed solidarity in creation and sin with Adam and solidarity in recreation and salvation with Christ. But how could these relationships be affirmed without effacing the personal distinctiveness of the parties? Here a crucial distinction was introduced between individual and generic humanity, between "the simple man and the universal man." Early in his career at Mercersburg, Nevin explained it in this fashion:

> Adam was not simply a man, like others since born, but he was the man, who comprehended in himself all that has since appeared in other men. Humanity as a whole resided in his person. He was strictly and truly the world. Through all ages, man is organically one and the same. And parallel with this precisely is the constitution of the Church. The second Adam corresponds in all respects with the first. He is not a man merely, an individual belonging to the race, but he is the man, emphatically the Son of Man, comprising in his person the new creation, or humanity recovered and redeemed as a whole.[12]

This generic identity was also understood in idealist and organic terms as a life principle or law that is communicated to those in union with the head—in the case of Adam this principle is natural while with Christ the principle is spiritual and supernatural. With the Incarnation a

11. See Torrance, "Karl Barth and the Latin Heresy."
12. Nevin, "Catholic Unity," 40.

new, spiritual principle has been introduced into human history, and while supernatural it nevertheless becomes integral with human existence. As Nevin put it, "The power of Christ's life lodged in the soul begins to work there immediately as the principle of the new creation. In doing so, it works organically according to the law which it includes in its own constitution. That is, it works as a human life; and as such becomes a law of regeneration in the body as truly as in the soul."[13]

By means of this distinction between individual and generic identity, then, the Mercersburg theologians believed they could affirm the realistic character of being in Adam and in Christ, and to do so without compromising individual identity. Once again, Nevin wrote, "*Such a relation of Christ to the Church involves no* UBIQUITY *or idealistic dissipation of his body, and requires no* FUSION *of his proper personality with the persons of his people.* We distinguish between the simple man and the universal man, here joined in the same person."[14]

Several comments are appropriate at this point. First, with this conception of generic humanity as determinative of the identity of those in solidarity with it, we begin to sense the profoundly corporate sensibility of Mercersburg. Nevin and his colleagues frequently condemned the nominalistic individualism popular in the America of his day, which reckoned humanity to be no more than a "sandheap" or the aggregate of individuals. For Mercersburg, the general precedes and conditions the individual—individual human beings are what they are by virtue of their union with Adam, and Christians are shaped by their solidarity with Christ. Second, in contrast to the natural/supernatural dualism axiomatic to much of the American Protestantism

13. Nevin, *Mystical Presence*, 172 (MTSS I, 153).
14. Ibid., 173 (MTSS I, 154).

of the day, we also sense a remarkable integrative impulse here. Yes, the natural and the supernatural are distinguished, but they do not finally stand in opposition to one another, and the supernatural can become integral to human existence. And third, the ultimate coherence of this notion of generic humanity and its relation to individual existence hangs on philosophical presuppositions that are broadly idealist and Platonic. For the Mercersburg theologians, this way of thinking owed much to the organic idealism of German philosophers such as Friedrich Schelling. In a description of T. F. Torrance's Christology that applies well to Mercersburg, George Hunsinger notes that the sanctified, generic humanity of Christ has "the status of a 'concrete universal.'"[15]

CHRIST AND THE SPIRIT

The supernatural character of Christ generic humanity is further explained in terms of its relationship to the Holy Spirit. How is it that this generic humanity becomes accessible to the human race? The answer given by Nevin is that Christ's humanity has been made spiritually accessible in that it has entered an eschatological form of existence that is conditioned by and imbued with the power of the Holy Spirit. As Nevin put it: "All is spiritual, glorious, heavenly. His whole humanity has been taken up into the sphere of the Spirit, and appears transfigured into the same life. And why then should it not extend itself, in the way of strict organic continuity, as a whole humanity also, by the active presence of Christ's Spirit, over into the persons of

15. Hunsinger, "The Dimension of Depth," 162. The Mercersburg affinity for Plato and the Christian Platonist tradition is helpfully explored by DiPuccio, "Nevin's Idealist Philosophy."

his people?"[16] This spiritualization of Christ's humanity, of course, entails no loss of corporeality, and the resurrection and ascension mark the "final triumph of the Spirit in the glorified humanity of Christ."[17] We are dealing here with a remarkable integration of Christology and pneumatology in service to the Mercersburg view of salvation.

Here we also see a sensitivity, remarkable for its time, to the unfolding of redemptive history in Scripture. The resurrection is not merely a proof of Christ's divinity (as many of Nevin's contemporaries apparently viewed it). Rather, it is integral to the accomplishing and the application of salvation. Moreover, the role of the Holy Spirit assumes a new character in light of Christ's resurrection and ascension. As Nevin wrote: "We read of God's Spirit as present with a certain kind of action in the world, before Christ came; but it will not do to take this as identical at all with the form of his presence in the world since. We are plainly told, that the Spirit as he now works in the Church, could not be given till Christ was glorified; the mystery of the incarnation must complete its course in his person, before room could be made for the farther revelation of its power in the other form."[18]

But here an interpretive question presents itself. Does this elevation and healing of Christ's fallen humanity take place by virtue of the Incarnation or by the work of the Holy Spirit? The answer seems to be that the change is due to both, although for all of Mercersburg's emphasis on the Incarnation, Nevin seems to stress even more the work of the Holy Spirit. It is by the work of the Holy Spirit that the Incarnation occurred; the resurrection itself was a work of the Spirit, and Christians are joined with Christ

16. Nevin, *Mystical Presence*, 176 (MTSS I, 156).

17. Ibid., 222 (MTSS I, 194).

18. Nevin, "Apostles' Creed," 330.

by the power of the Spirit. Here Nevin appeals to the peri-choresis or interpenetration of the divine persons—"They subsist in the way of the most perfect mutual inbeing and intercommunion"[19]—and thus it is safe to say that Mercersburg had a robust and developed doctrine of the Holy Spirit or pneumatology to go along with its Christology.

SALVATION IN CHRIST

The Mercersburg view of salvation flows from this Christology. The key theme here is union with Christ, the real participation of the Christian in Christ's life and redemptive work. "Christianity," Nevin declared, "is grounded in the living union of the believer with the person of Christ."[20] This "living union" is framed, in context, over against two foils. It is deeper than the "moral union" promoted by the evangelical New England successors of Jonathan Edwards, who viewed the Christian's relationship with Christ as little more than voluntary agreement and a sharing of moral concern. Such a perspective tends to reduce the essence of religion to morality and often leads to a sterile legalism. At the same time, this living union with Christ is distinguished from the abstract conception that prevailed in later Reformed Orthodoxy with its forensic preoccupation. For example, at the Princeton Seminary in which Nevin was trained, the Christian's relationship to Christ was framed along two dissimilar lines—a legal, extrinsic, forensic union with Christ construed in nominalist terms that resulted in justification and the immediate imputation of Christ's righteousness to the Christian on the one hand, and a sanctifying presence of the Holy Spirit, who served as a sort of surrogate for Christ in heaven, on the other. Both of these

19. Nevin, *Mystical Presence*, 225 (MTSS I, 196).
20. Ibid., 51 (MTSS I, 40).

options were viewed by the Mercersburg theologians as too abstract and external. Neither affirmed a realistic union with the incarnate Christ.

In contrast to New England Calvinism and the federal theology of Princeton, Mercersburg sought to frame union in terms of a real and mystical union that connected the humanity of the believer with the incarnate humanity of Christ in heaven.[21] As Nevin put it in his sermon on "Catholic Unity,"

> This may sound mystical; but, after all, it is no more difficult to comprehend than the fact of our union to the same extent with the person of the first Adam. As descended from him by natural generation, we are not only like him in outward form and inward spirit, but we participate truly and properly in his very nature. We are members of his body, of his flesh, and of his bones. His humanity, soul and body, has passed over into our persons. And so it is in the case of the second Adam, as it regards the truly regenerate. They are inserted into his life, through faith, by the power of the Holy Ghost . . . The whole humanity of Christ, soul and body, is carried over by the process of the Christian salvation into the person of the believer, so that in the end his glorified body, no less than his glorified soul, will appear as the natural and necessary product of the life in which he is thus made to participate.[22]

Here, of course, Nevin was echoing the Reformer John Calvin's emphasis on union with the "substance" of Christ's humanity by faith and the power of the Holy Spirit, and

21. For a detailed analysis of these debates, see Evans, *Imputation and Impartation*.

22. Nevin, "Catholic Unity," 38–39.

Mercersburg was deeply suspicious of any salvation scheme that neglected to affirm the deep and abiding connection between Christ and the Christian, and failed to recognize that the benefits of salvation are inseparable from the person of Christ.

> A very common view appears to be, that the whole salvation of the gospel is accomplished, in a more or less outward and mechanical way, by supernatural might and power, rather than by the Spirit of the Lord as the revelation of a new historical life in the person of the believer himself. So we have an outward imputation of righteousness to begin with; a process of sanctification carried forward by the help of proper spiritual machinery brought to bear on the soul, including perhaps, as its basis, the notion of an abrupt creation *de novo*, by the fiat of the Holy Ghost; and finally, to crown all, a sudden unprepared refabrication of the body, as an entirely new product of Almighty power at the moment, to be superadded to the life of the spirit already complete in its state of glory. But the Scriptures sanction no such hypothesis in the case . . . It is a new creation in Christ Jesus, not by him in the way of mere outward power.[23]

The sacramental implications of this view of salvation were, of course, substantial, and these will be explored in the next chapter.

JUSTIFICATION AND SANCTIFICATION

Since the Reformation, Protestants, especially in the Reformed tradition, had often described salvation in a twofold fashion as involving both justification by faith

23. Nevin, *Mystical Presence*, 228 (MTSS I, 198).

(an acceptance by God not based upon good works) and sanctification or transformation of life, with both essential but in different ways. Thus Calvin spoke of a *duplex gratia*, or "double grace," that flows from that saving union: "By partaking of him, we principally receive a double grace: namely, that being reconciled to God through Christ's blamelessness, we may have in heaven instead of a Judge a gracious Father; and secondly, that sanctified by Christ's Spirit we may cultivate blamelessness and purity of life."[24] The benefits or blessings of salvation are framed by Mercersburg in this typically twofold Protestant fashion, albeit with some interesting twists that reveal some differences between the two key figures in the movement, Nevin and Schaff.

Sanctification is treated in in conventional Protestant and Reformed terms. It is a lifelong process (Mercersburg had little use for the Wesleyan notion of perfection attainable in this life) that is furthered by the means of grace, especially the preaching of the word and the sacraments, as these are encountered in the life of the church. It is rooted in the believer's union with Christ, which in this context is seen as the infusion of the very life of Christ: "The new life lodges itself, as an efflux from Christ, in the inmost core of our personality. Here it becomes the principle or seed of our sanctification; which is simply the gradual transfusion of the same exalted spiritual quality or potence through our whole persons."[25]

It is in the area of justification, what Schaff had termed the "material principle of the Reformation," that differences emerge. Philip Schaff's description of this doctrine in *The*

24. Calvin, *Institutes*, III.11.1. On Calvin's view of union with Christ, see Evans, *Imputation and Impartation*, 7–41; Garcia, *Life in Christ*; Canlis, *Calvin's Ladder*.

25. Nevin, *Mystical Presence*, 168 (MTSS I, 149).

Principle of Protestantism is a good place to start, and it is remarkable for its conventionally Protestant character. The doctrine is set in opposition to all Pelagian or semi-Pelagian self-righteousness (as reflected, e.g., in Roman Catholic synergism). The merit of Christ is the only ground of justification, and faith is the instrumental cause. Justification consists in the forgiveness of sins and the imputation of the righteousness of Christ to the believer, and the faith that receives Christ involves not only assent but also heartfelt trust. All this is textbook Protestantism. The only mildly innovative move here, in response to the objection that such justification is a legal fiction, is Schaff's viewing the decree of justification as a creative act by which the "principle of righteousness" (that is, Christ himself) is actualized in the believer.[26]

Turning to John W. Nevin, the picture becomes more complex. In some contrast to Schaff, Nevin insisted that justification had been overemphasized in recent Protestantism, and he was clearly concerned about how some had taken this emphasis on justification in an antinomian direction. But Nevin's deeper concern was the abstraction of the doctrine from the persons involved. He was convinced that many in his day framed the doctrine in a completely extrinsic way. "The tendency," he told his students at Mercersburg, "is to over-emphasize the external side of the transaction and to ignore the internal or organic relation."[27] In other words, Nevin was deeply concerned that people were trying to understand justification without reference to the believer's union with Christ!

To be sure, there is much that is conventionally Protestant in Nevin's view of justification. Justification is by faith

26. See Schaff, *Principle of Protestantism*, 80–97 (MTSS III, 79–94).

27. Erb, *Nevin's Theology*, 203.

and involves both forgiveness of sins and the imputation of Christ's righteousness. But certain factors in Nevin's thinking create dissonance with Reformational thought. First, he embraced the common eighteenth and nineteenth-century moral-philosophy assumption that merit and demerit inhere in persons and cannot be abstracted from personality. By itself this was not a major problem, but he also believed that there was a precise parallel between hamartiological and soteriological imputation. Adam's offspring, according to Nevin, are accounted as sinners because they participate in his sinful condition, and likewise those united with Christ are accounted righteous because they participate in his righteousness. Nevin wrote: "The moral relations of Adam, and his moral character too, are made over to us at the same time. Our participation in the actual unrighteousness of his life, forms the ground of our participation in his guilt and liability to punishment. And in no other way, we affirm, can the idea of imputation be satisfactorily sustained in the case of the second Adam. The scriptures make the two cases, in this respect, fully parallel."[28] This is, to use seventeenth-century scholastic categories, mediate imputation (i.e., imputation through participation in a moral quality). In contrast, Luther and Calvin clearly affirmed the justification of the ungodly (recall Luther's famous *simul iustus et peccator*, the Christian as simultaneously justified and a sinner), what nineteenth-century theologians termed a "synthetic justification" (i.e., a justification not in accordance with the facts, and in contrast to an analytic justification that was in accordance with the actual facts). But Nevin speaks in terms of what is really a proleptic and analytic justification. God declares the sinner righteous because they are (or at least will be) righteous. Nevin writes in *The Mystical Presence*:

28. Nevin, *Mystical Presence*, 190–91 (MTSS I, 167–68).

> The judgment of God must ever be according to truth. He cannot reckon to anyone an attribute or quality, which does not belong to him in fact. He cannot declare him to be in a relation or state, which is not actually his own, but the position merely of another . . . The law in this view would be itself a fiction only, and not the expression of a fact. But no such fiction, whether under the name of law or without it, can lie at the ground of a judgment entertained or pronounced by God.[29]

Nevin also expanded the definition of faith to include works of evangelical obedience. Seeking to reconcile Paul and James, Nevin told his students: "There is no great difficulty in reconciling them, if we keep in view what Paul means by faith. He always takes it as a life, necessarily including other affections and graces, such as love and hope, as well as corresponding outward acts."[30] While there is Protestant precedent for this move (most notably in Jonathan Edwards and his successors[31]), it does sound rather "Catholic," and the concerns widely expressed about Mercersburg's "catholicizing" on this matter were not entirely without foundation.

THE RATIONALE OF THE INCARNATION

One final question—and one with considerable relevance for understanding Mercersburg's relationship to German philosophy—has to do with whether the Incarnation would have occurred apart from sin. Nevin insisted that the

29. Ibid., 189 (MTSS I, 166).

30. Erb, *Nevin's Theology*, 306.

31. See Evans, *Imputation and Impartation*, 107–111, 124, 257–58.

Incarnation is much more than a mere precondition for the Atonement: "The true order is, the mystery of the Incarnation first, and then the atonement, as growing forth from this."[32] Such statements could imply, though they probably do not necessitate, that the Incarnation would have occurred even apart from sin. Further complicating the issue is the fact that the Mercersburg theologians were the heirs of German organic idealism as it came to them through the Mediating Theologians. According to this way of thinking, the Incarnation is the *telos* or goal of creation in which the idea of divine–human unity is finally realized. Consistent with this, Nevin can argue, "The nature of the Messianic idea has its necessity in the constitution of humanity,"[33] and here an ontological necessity of the Incarnation even apart from sin seems to be implied.

Nevin engaged this question in two lengthy reviews of German works—by Karl Theodor Albert Liebner and Julius Müller—that appeared in the *Mercersburg Review* in 1851.[34] In the first, Nevin recounts the arguments of Liebner for the necessity of the Incarnation apart from sin. In the second, Nevin summarizes the case made by Julius Müller for the hamartiological rationale. Müller's case was formidable in its marshaling of biblical evidence, and more impressive still was his presentation of what he took to be the implications of Liebner's view—a confusion of the moral and the metaphysical, a subversion of the freedom of God, and tendencies toward pantheism and universalism. Nevin was taken aback by this, and did not pass final judgment on the matter.[35]

32. Nevin, "Apostles' Creed," 343.

33. Erb, *Nevin's Theology*, 236.

34. See Nevin, "Liebner's Christology"; "*Cur Deus Homo*" (MTSS IV, 87–135).

35. Nevin's indecision on this point is fascinating. Nichols,

That being said, however, the heart of Nevin's positive argument for the Incarnation—that the Logos had been united with fallen human nature, had sanctified it, and thus had raised humanity to a new level of existence—was, in fact, compatible with either rationale for the Incarnation. And this, in turn, raises a further set of questions that cut to the heart of our understanding of Nevin as a theologian, and of the broader Mercersburg movement. This author was written elsewhere: "Is Nevin to be understood primarily as an idealist theologian in the tradition of the German mediating theologians? Or is he better seen as a biblical theologian with deep patristic and Reformation roots, who found the apparatus of German idealism useful in providing an idiom for articulating certain concerns but who was not slavishly devoted to that apparatus when there were reasons to diverge from it? On balance, the latter interpretation seems better to fit the facts."[36] A careful survey of the biblical citations in the Mercersburg theology materials provides strong testimony to just how *scriptural* they were, and Nevin's failure to defend an obvious implication of the idealist Christology against Müller's learned onslaught at least suggests a measure of independence.

QUESTIONS

1. Why did the Mercersburg theologians speak of Jesus Christ as "the Second Adam"?

Romanticism in American Theology, pp. 149–50, wonders, "Did he hang on dead center, unready to decide? Was he already feeling the paralysis of will which was shortly to cripple his speculative interest? This whole aspect of the Mercersburg Christology ran into a question mark and remained unresolved."

36. Evans, "Mercersburg Christology and Reformed *Ressourcement*," 399.

2. In what ways did the church father Irenaeus influence the Mercersburg theologians?

3. What did Nevin mean by "generic humanity"?

4. How is the theme of "union with Christ" central to the Mercersburg understanding of salvation?

5

HISTORY AND THE NATURE OF THE CHURCH

THE CHRISTOLOGICAL FOCUS OUTLINED in the previous chapter and the movement's corporate sensibility carry over powerfully into the Mercersburg view of the church. The church is the body of Christ, the sphere of salvation, the place where the very life of Christ is manifested in and through those united with him. Christ and church are correlates, and Nevin even echoed some Anglican theologians of the day by speaking of the church as the continuation of the Incarnation on earth, the mode of Christ's presence here: "Christ himself is made perfect in the Church, as the head in our natural organization requires the body in order to its completion. There can be no Church without

Christ, but we may reverse the proposition also and say, no Church, no Christ."[1]

In Mercersburg we also find a deep suspicion of "abstract" or "mechanical" conceptions of the church that viewed it as a mere voluntary society or sum of its constituent parts. As we noted earlier, Nevin often used the disparaging term "sand-heap" in these contexts. Rather, the general must precede the particular, the whole the individual parts: "The Church does not rest upon its members, but the members rest upon the Church. Individual Christianity is not something older than general Christianity, but the general in this case goes before the particular, and rules and conditions all its manifestations. So it is with every organic nature."[2] Nevin further illustrated this priority of the general over the particular by distinguishing between the terms *all* and *whole*. *All* denotes a "mechanical unity" made up of "parts," while *whole* suggests an "organic unity, where the parts as such have no separate and independent existence."[3]

HISTORICAL DEVELOPMENT

Another key element of the Mercersburg ecclesiology, or view of the church, is its conception of historical development. This theme was particularly highlighted, as we have seen, in Schaff's *Principle of Protestantism*, but it pervades the Mercersburg writings. Nevin sought to express this notion of ecclesial development with a key distinction. First there is the "ideal church," which is "the power of a new supernatural creation, which has been introduced into the actual history of the world by the Incarnation of Jesus Christ." This ideal church, furthermore, is "a living system,

1. Nevin, "The Church," 66.
2. Nevin, "Catholic Unity," 40.
3. Nevin, "Catholicism," 3 (MTSS VII, 13).

organically bound together in all its parts, springing from a common ground, and pervaded throughout with the force of a common nature."[4] Second, there is the "actual church," the ideal church as it manifests itself in history, and Nevin notes that "the history of the actual Church, then, is but the presence and life of the Ideal Church itself, struggling through a process of centuries to come to its last, full manifestation."[5] The actual church, however, falls short of fully realizing the ideal, and this is how Nevin accounts for the defects evident at all stages of church history.

Historian David Layman has noted how two distinct, albeit closely related, conceptualities are used here. First, the church is seen as a living, *organic* reality, and as such something that is dynamic, that grows. This organic conception of the church is, of course, an implication of the Mercersburg soteriology. Christianity, Nevin maintained, is a life and not a doctrine; the very life of Christ is motivating and transforming the church, and so the church will evince this life dynamic in its history. The second theme is that of idealist-influenced dialectical development, a way of thinking that provided a sense of shape and direction or teleology to this organic process. The key figure here was Philip Schaff, who had studied under idealist historians such as F. C. Baur and August Neander in Germany. Baur had famously schematized the development of early Christianity in Hegelian fashion as the thesis of Petrine Jewish Christianity meeting the antithesis of Pauline Gentile Christianity and issuing in the synthesis of the Old Catholic Church, while Neander had sought to explicate the unfolding inner logic of the church over time. In addition, the philosopher Friedrich Schelling in his later period had presented the dialectical development of the church through Petrine

4. Nevin, "The Church," 58–59.

5. Ibid., 64.

(Catholic) and Pauline (Protestant) stages, and he looked forward to a third stage of Johannine Christianity that would preserve the best aspects of both earlier stages.

Schaff often sought to uncover this teleology in his historical writing, and the significance of this should not be underestimated. Layman has gone so far as to describe the Mercersburg Theology as "defined by this synthesis of Nevin's organicism and Schaff's developmentalism," and Layman goes on to argue plausibly that Nevin later rejected Schaff's more teleological conception of development and returned to his earlier notion of organic change.[6] This may, in fact, provide the best explanation of "Nevin's dizziness." It was one thing to affirm a dynamic view of church history (as Nevin did early on), but it was another to argue that new stages dialectically preserve what is best about what precedes them. Here Nevin was in a bind, for the American Protestantism of his day seemed to repudiate what he deemed best about the Catholic past, and that didn't look like progress!

Two important implications of this dynamic, developmental approach should be noted. First, in contrast to the "apostasy theory" of church history then espoused by much of American Protestantism, that viewed the period between the New Testament and the Reformation as a spiritual "Dark Ages," Mercersburg had a much higher appraisal of medieval Roman Catholicism. As Nevin put it in 1849, "There is no escape then from the consequence that God was with the Church through the middle ages, gloriously carrying forward by its means the vast problem of christianity, with

---

6. Layman, "General Introduction," in *Born of Water and the Spirit*, 24, 31. DiPuccio, *Interior Sense of Scripture*, 85, also recognizes Nevin's disenchantment with the notion of positive historical development.

steady progress, towards its appointed end.[7] This conception of development also meant that the Reformation was not the last word—there is room for further development. Schaff identified the "diseases of Protestantism" as rationalism and sectarianism, both of which were symptoms of an undue focus on subjectivity, and he looked forward to a time when the excesses of both Catholicism and Protestantism would be transcended by a higher synthesis.[8]

Second, this approach involved a rejection of the distinction between the visible and the invisible church that had been enshrined in Reformed Protestant theology since the sixteenth century. For Calvin and the Westminster Assembly, the invisible church is made up of the elect chosen by God from all eternity, while the visible church is those who profess Christian faith and their children, the church as it outwardly appears on earth. In this fashion the Reformers sought to explain how the church as it is presently experienced is defective in various ways and a mixture of saints and sinners. In other words, for much Reformed theology the visible church is an imperfect approximation of the invisible, which sooner or later almost inevitably raises the question of whether the visible church is really the church at all. But for Mercersburg, this distinction was abstract and tended undercut belief in the church as it is concretely experienced: "An absolutely invisible Church can never be apprehended as a true Church."[9] And so Nevin insisted that the Ideal and the Actual Church are inseparable, that the second is but the first coming to expression in history: "It is neither the Ideal Church, of course, nor the actual Church,

7. Nevin, "True and False Protestantism," 92. See also Schaff, *Principle of Protestantism*, 59–74 (MTSS III, 63–75).

8. Schaff, *Principle of Protestantism*, 129–155 (MTSS III, 119–41).

9. Nevin, "The Church," 68.

separately taken, that forms the proper object of our faith, as expressed in the Creed, but the first as comprehended always in the second, and constituting with it the presence of a single life . . . As such, it is a visible, catholic, historical, and life bearing Church, and is to be embraced in the way of faith accordingly."[10]

AUTHORITY IN THE CHURCH

The Mercersburg theologians were confronted by a pressing crisis of churchly authority in the form of American sectarianism. In America, traditionally Protestant doctrines of *sola Scriptura* (Scripture alone as the final authority for the Christian) and the Christian's right of "private judgment" to interpret the Bible for himself or herself were given free rein, and the result, particularly on the frontier, was an explosion of denominations and sects, each claiming that its reading of Scripture was correct. Nevin wrote:

> It all sounds well, to lay so much stress on the authority of the Bible, as the only text-book and guide of Christianity. But what are we to think of it, when we find such a motley mass of protesting systems, all laying claim so vigorously here to one and the same watchword . . . However plausible it may be in theory, to magnify in such style the unbound use solely of the Bible for the adjustment of Christian faith and practice the simple truth is, that the operation of it in fact is, not to unite the church into one, but to divide it always more and more into sects.[11]

The deeper question, Nevin and Schaff realized, was how should Scripture be read and interpreted? It was one

10. Ibid., 67.

11. Nevin, "Sect System," 491 (*Catholic and Reformed*, 137–38).

thing for Luther and Calvin to assert the principle of *Sola Scriptura* with the Bible as self-authenticating and self-interpreting in their sixteenth-century context of robust ecclesiology and learned exegesis—both of which set fairly clear limits on interpretation. But when the notion of Scripture alone was imported into the context of American individualism, democratization, and populism those boundaries became anything but clear, and a plethora of sects was the result.

Nevin and Schaff well realized that truism of late modernity and post-modernity: interpretation is inevitable; we don't simply read Scripture in a common-sense fashion and directly apprehend its meaning. And this interpretive process is complicated; pre-understanding is important. What sort of presuppositions will lead to appropriate and meaningful interpretation? One of Nevin's more compelling points in "The Sect System" is that these groups, while claiming to just be reading the Bible, were actually reading Scripture through their own lenses. Furthermore, there was the problem of justifying this preunderstanding, which could easily degenerate into a heteronomous exercise, either in the form of the magisterium of Roman Catholicism or the cult of personality of sectarian leaders—both of which appealed to a bald, external authority. As Nevin put it, "The liberty of the sects consists at last, in thinking its particular notions, shouting its shibboleths and passwords, dancing to its religious hornpipes, and reading the Bible only through its theological goggles. These restrictions, at the same time, are so many wires, that lead back at last into the hands of a few leading spirits, enabling them to wield a true hierarchical despotism over all who are thus brought within their power."[12]

12. Ibid., 498 (*Catholic and Reformed*, 144).

But what theological pre-understanding will enable people to read Scripture rightly and without simply reducing to an appeal to external authority? Key here is the nature of faith and the role of that faith in the interpretive process. The Mercersburg theologians were convinced that the Christian's union by faith and the Holy Spirit with Christ, a participation in the very divine–human life of Christ, is more fundamental than both doctrine and piety, and that faith therefore precedes understanding.[13] Christian faith, for Mercersburg, involves an apprehension in consciousness of spiritual realities and a union with its object. Just as the sense of vision enables one to perceive physical objects, so faith is "the organ by which we perceive and apprehend the spiritual and the eternal."[14] Moreover, it is neither mere blind assent to an external, mechanical authority nor the result of reasoning one's way to faith or "ratiocination." With Mercersburg's sustained polemic against the external and abstract, the common view of faith in American Protestantism as assent to rational truths was unattractive. Nevin wrote, "Faith carries in its very nature its own warrant and guaranty. It is the 'substance and evidence' of the realities it brings into view. Thus related to its object, it is no blind assent of course to mere outward authority. Just as little, however, can it be regarded as the product of ratiocination."[15] Here Nevin and Schaff were tapping into that rich Augustinian and Anselmian tradition of Christian Platonism. If theology and exegesis are matters of *fides quaerens intellectum*, or "faith seeking understanding," then theology and biblical interpretation are to be done from within the circle of faith. And that circle of

13. See Nevin, "Review of God in Christ," 312; Nevin, "Apostles' Creed," 207, 211, 345.

14. Nevin, "Apostles' Creed," 208.

15. Ibid., 206.

faith is described in the creedal tradition of the Church, and especially in the Apostles' Creed. In light of this, it is not surprising that Nevin had little use for attempts to rationally prove the Christian faith by historical evidences of the resurrection and so forth.

But how is this appeal to the tradition of the church as it is enshrined in the Apostles' Creed not to be viewed as an appeal to bald external authority? Here Nevin argued that the Creed was "no work of mere outward *authority*, imposed on the Church by Christ or his Apostles." Rather, it is "the direct utterance of Christian faith itself."[16] It arose organically as the expression of Christian identity and consciousness in response to the revelation of the incarnate Christ. Nevin wrote,

> So in the case before us, that the first christian symbol, the Apostles' Creed, should not spring from any particular source or authorship, but come down to us rather as the free spontaneous product of the life of the Church as a whole, the self-adjusted utterance of its faith, we may say, as it was felt to have stood from time immemorial; that no one can show exactly when or how it rose, and took its present shape; that its origin, in one work, is not mathematically definite, but confused and vague, and referable to no fixed time or place; all this, to our mind, is just as it ought to be, and rightly considered invests it with the highest title it could well have to our confidence and respect. It is in this character precisely of its organic relation to the life of christianity as a whole, that its authority maybe said primarily and mainly to stand.[17]

16. Ibid., 201, 205.
17. Ibid., 218.

And what is the relation of this church tradition to the Bible? This was a particularly pressing question for the Mercersburg theologians as Protestants with their inherited tradition of *sola Scriptura*, or "Scripture alone" as the final authority for the Christian. Mercersburg clearly assigned a greater place to the tradition of the church than most Protestants of the day, and the reasons for this were both hermeneutical and Christological. Nevin did not want the Scriptures to overshadow Christ; moreover, he realized that preunderstanding is inevitable and that in the absence of an agreed upon approach to Scripture the interpretive process will degenerate into chaos.

> The Bible is not the principle of Christianity, nor its foundation; this is a fact, out of the New Testament, before it and beyond it, which has its *principium* in the living person of Christ; and which, in this form, must rule the interpretation of the Bible for every true believer, and not be itself ruled, through the Bible, simply by his own mind . . . And yet, in the face of it, what becomes of all this talk about private judgment and the Bible, as the sole factors of the christian faith? Christianity itself, as something far more than any private judgment, must assist me to the true sense of the Scriptures, or I shall study them to little purpose . . . The question, then, is not, whether the Bible shall be our sole rule of faith, but with what inward posture and habit we are to come to the study of the Bible for this purpose; for it is grossly absurd to suppose, that we can ever come to it without *some* such posture and habit.[18]

For Nevin, the tradition of the church as expressed, for example, in the Apostles' Creed is in a sense more

18. Nevin, "Puritanism and the Creed," 598–99.

fundamental than the Bible for Christianity. Tradition is not merely derived from Scripture; rather, both tradition and Scripture arise from the "original substance of Christianity itself," and this tradition "becomes the living stream into which continuously the sense of the Bible is poured, through the Holy Ghost, from age to age."[19] This parallelism of tradition and Scripture would seem, on the face of it, to require a different view of inspiration than Nevin was taught at Princeton, and later in his career Nevin bemoaned the "mechanical" and "abstract" view of inspiration that saw only an "external" relationship between the divine and human. And so, using language that would seem to anticipate Karl Barth, Nevin asserts that the Bible "is no longer taken to be identical with revelation itself. It is not its very principle and fountain, but only its documentary record. To be this, it must, of course, be inspired. But the inspiration of the record is not, in and of itself, the origin of what is thus divinely attested and made known."[20]

But unlike Barth, Nevin's concerns at this point were motivated, not by the findings of the emerging biblical criticism (his views on such matters remained quite conservative), but rather by the sense that the older view he had been taught saw Scripture as merely the outward communication of doctrines and ideas to more or less passive human beings, doctrines and ideas whose meaning could be ascertained by grammatical-historical exegesis (that is, figuring out what the language meant in its original human context). But Nevin found all this deeply unsatisfying, for he sensed that if the divine had truly entered human history, the meaning of Scripture would inevitably transcend the merely human. And so he was more open than many of his American contemporaries, with their "common-sense"

19. Nevin, "Apostles' Creed," 339.
20. Nevin, *My Own Life*, 50.

hermeneutic, to the mystical dimension of Scripture and to multiple levels of meaning.[21] He also well knew that such *sensus plenior* or "fuller sense" interpretation had been the norm for most of Christian history.[22]

Thus it might appear, if we follow Nevin in particular, that Mercersburg rather decisively subordinates the interpretation of Scripture to the tradition of the Church. But here we detect a measure of difference between Nevin and Philip Schaff. Schaff certainly affirmed the indispensability of tradition, but he also contended that the *regula fidei* or "rule of faith" as expressed in the great creeds of the church is "not a part of the divine word separately from that which is written, but the contents of scripture itself as apprehended and settled by the church against heresies past and always new appearing; not an independent source of revelation, but the one fountain of the written word, only rolling itself forward in the stream of church consciousness."[23] So, far from setting the tradition of the church over against Scripture, Schaff actually subordinates it to Scripture in a manner that sounds authentically Protestant and Reformational. Once again we see that Nevin tended to be more "catholic" and Schaff more "protestant."

THE SACRAMENTS IN THE CHURCH

The Mercersburg Theology was notable for its sacramental concern—an emphasis that placed it at odds with much of nineteenth-century American Protestantism. J. H. Nichols was doubtless correct in observing, "The Mercersburg

21. See Nevin, *My Own Life*, 48–56, 128–38. See also Nevin, "Internal Sense of Holy Scripture."

22. On this larger issue, see Steinmetz, "Superiority of Pre-Critical Exegesis"; Carter, *Interpreting Scripture with the Great Tradition*.

23. Schaff, *Principle of Protestantism*, 116 (MTSS III, 109–10).

movement might be called essentially a sacramental, more particularly a Eucharistic, revival."[24] All the Mercersburg theologians were convinced that the sacraments actually do something; to use the language of traditional Reformed theology, they are real "means of grace." In terms of Reformation antecedents, Mercersburg stood much closer to the robust sacramentalism of Calvin and Luther than to the spiritual subjectivism of the Swiss Reformer Zwingli, who denied that physical things could be instruments of divine grace.[25] When Nevin came to Mercersburg, Zwingli's memorialism, which held that the Supper is little more than a mental exercise in recollection, was being touted by many as the proper heritage of the German Reformed Church, and Nevin's recovery of the authentic Calvinistic view of the true presence of Christ in the Lord's Supper created quite a stir.

Nevin defined a sacrament in conventional older Protestant terms as an outward visible sign and an inward grace, and he insisted on the "sacramental" connection between the sign and the thing signified. Baptism signifies union with Christ and this union actually takes place; the Lord's Supper is a real communication of the incarnate humanity of Christ to the believer. This notion of a sacrament was, of course, framed over against the popular American Protestant conception of baptism and the Lord's Supper as "ordinances," or things that one does in accordance with divine command. Nevin wrote,

> A sacrament in the true church sense is not a mere outward rite, made obligatory by divine appointment. It carries in itself a peculiar constitution of its own. It consists, according to the old definition, of two parts, one outward and the

24. Nichols, *Romanticism in American Theology*, 84.

25. See Zwingli, "On the Lord's Supper."

other inward, a visible terrene sign and an invisible celestial grace; not related simply as corresponding facts, brought together by human thought; but the one actually bound to the other in the way of most real mystical or sacramental union, causing the last to be objectively at hand in one and the same transaction with the first.[26]

But the Mercersburg sacramentology did not fit without remainder into the older Protestant wineskins. While Calvin had viewed the sacraments as concessions, albeit important and necessary concessions, to human weakness, Nevin saw them as essential and fundamental: "Baptism and the Lord's Supper are the central institutions of Christianity."[27] Furthermore, Nevin's sacramental sensibility went considerably deeper than the traditional Reformed focus on the means of grace. In fact, his conception of reality in general was profoundly sacramental. As Nevin told his students, "The whole constitution of the world is sacramental, as being not simply the sign of, but the actual form and presence of invisible things."[28] Here he approaches what contemporary Roman Catholic theologian David Tracy has called the "Catholic analogical imagination." As Tracy describes it, "We literally reimagine reality as a new series of ordered possibilities; we then choose some central clue for the whole of reality—for Catholics that central clue to the whole—to the relationship between God and humanity, the individual and society—is found in what T. S. Eliot called the half-guessed, the gift—half-understood—incarnation as the secret of both God and humankind and the relationship of both church and cosmos as finally sacramental."[29]

26. Nevin, "Noel on Baptism," 243–44 (MTSS VI, 94–95).
27. Erb, *Nevin's Theology*, 372.
28. Ibid., 373.
29. Tracy, "Catholic Analogical Imagination," 236.

This sacramental focus also had implications for the place of the relationship of word and sacrament. The Word written and preached is not as central for Mercersburg as it was for Luther and Calvin. Nevin writes, "the sacraments as means for the application of redemption have a certain priority over the Word, which has power to reach us only as we stand in proper relation to God by the sacraments."[30] Of course, this sacramental focus of Mercersburg cannot be properly understood apart from its deeply incarnational center—the written Word is important, but subordinate to the incarnate Word of God, Jesus Christ, and for Nevin the relationship of union with Christ is established and furthered primarily by the sacraments.

Baptism presented, for a variety of reasons, a considerable challenge to Nevin as he sought to reconcile his notions of sacramental efficacy with his Protestant heritage. He insisted that baptism is more than a mere sign; it is the means whereby a person enters into salvation: "Most clearly in the New Testament, it is made to enter efficaciously, as a divine act, into the mystery of the new birth . . . Baptism here is no mere sign, no simply outward adjunct or accident. It is the washing of regeneration; it saves us; it is for the remission of sins."[31] Nevin's patristic studies had convinced him that belief in baptismal grace had been present from the beginning of the Christian movement, and that a proper understanding of the church hinged upon it: "The true issue in the end is this: Church or No-Church; sacrament or mere moral sign."[32]

This emphasis on sacramental objectivity is evident in Nevin's argument for infant baptism. Particularly interesting is how Nevin does *not* argue for the baptism of infants.

30. Erb, *Nevin's Theology*, 285.

31. Nevin, "Noel on Baptism," 245 (MTSS VI, 95–96).

32. Ibid., 258 (MTSS VI, 109).

Largely absent is the older Reformed argument for infant baptism as a covenant sign that had been initially framed by Zwingli, further developed by Calvin, and enshrined in Reformed confessional documents such as the Westminster Confession of Faith. This argument held that circumcision was the sign of the covenant of grace in the Old Testament dispensation and baptism the sign of that same covenant of grace in the New Testament dispensation, and that just as infants were given the sign of circumcision, so also the infant children of believers should be baptized. But for Nevin, the "use of infant baptism in particular turns altogether on the assumption of such an objective force in the ordinance, and must be surely undermined indeed, sooner or later, wherever this assumption is renounced."[33] In addition, Nevin also rejected efforts to proof-text the practice of infant baptism from Scripture. For Nevin, the rationale for baptizing infants arises, not from isolated biblical texts mechanically interpreted, but from Christian consciousness of the nature of Christianity itself as it is conditioned by the Incarnation. Here he presents an Irenaean, second-Adam argument that Christ came to redeem humanity at all stages of its development—the young as well as the mature: "Only in the character of a grace-bearing sacrament, according to the view taken of it by the early Church, and only in connection with the idea of an objective salvation in Christ commensurate with the entire tract of our human life from infancy to old age, can baptism be vindicated rationally as the proper privilege of infants. Renounce this old theory of Christianity, and it is no longer possible to make any satisfactory stand here against the plausible reasonings of the Baptists."[34]

33. Nevin, "Anglican Crisis," 370.
34. Nevin, "Noel on Baptism," 261 (MTSS VI, 111).

Nevertheless, Nevin struggled as he sought to explain what baptism actually does, candidly admitting that "there are great difficulties attending the subject of baptismal grace."[35] Baptism removes the curse of original sin but the grace of baptism can be lost because of later sin (here Nevin comes rather close to the Roman Catholic position as it was codified at the Council of Trent in the Counter-Reformation period).[36] But Nevin's insistence on the objective efficacy of the sacrament created friction at two closely related points—the necessity of faith and the centrality of union with Christ by faith. Given the traditional Reformed insistence on faith as essential for mystical union and justification, how can infants experience salvation when faith (understood by Nevin as a state of self-consciousness) is impossible? Nevin does not develop a theory of infant faith, and this dilemma is evident in his 1851 theological lectures. There Nevin hints at what this writer has termed Calvin's "offer-reception" theory of sacramental efficacy, in which what baptism and the Lord's Supper objectively offer must be subjectively received by faith. Nevin told his students:

> How is it with infants who cannot exercise faith? They are united to their parents. However, the value or objective force of baptism does not depend on the faith of the parents or even of the officiating minister. It is the act of Christ and has its force in His fidelity. The force, however, cannot take effect without the conditions that follow. But if we can distinguish between objective and subjective in the case of adults, then, also, there must be a distinction in the case of infants. In the case of adults, objective and subjective fall together; in the case of infants they fall apart.

35. Ibid., 265 (MTSS VI, 114).
36. See Erb, *Nevin's Theology*, 390.

> The objective may have place and be of force in
> infants, and yet take place in the future. This is
> what is meant, or what should be meant, by the
> phrase, "baptismal regeneration."[37]

Here we sense that Nevin's thinking was not fully
formed, and that he was caught to some degree between
his Protestant heritage and his patristic studies of the old
Catholic tradition. On balance, he seems less concerned to
codify precisely the nature of baptismal efficacy as salvific
in any final sense and more concerned to present baptism
as effectively and objectively the beginning of the Christian
life: "The old catholic faith, with its ideas of sacramental
grace and educational sanctification, the powers of heaven
underlying and supporting the process of piety in a real
way, through the Church, from the hour of baptism onward
to the hour of death, as compared with this, may well seem
like the land of Beulah, full of green pastures and springs,
in contrast with a wilderness of sand."[38] This emphasis on
"educational religion" and the lack of a doctrine of infant
faith also explain Nevin's rejection of the practice of infant
communion and his insistence on the rite of confirmation:
"Infant baptism assumes the possibility of educational religion . . . and looks to it as its own necessary complement.
The idea of confirmation is required to bring it to its true
and full sense."[39]

The question of baptismal efficacy was directly addressed by E. V. Gerhart in an extended 1858 essay in the
Mercersburg Review, which was occasioned by Presbyterian
discussions bemoaning the fact that a large percentage of
Presbyterian children remained unbaptized.[40] Gerhart ar-

---

37. Erb, *Nevin's Theology*, 390.

38. Nevin, "Noel on Baptism," 252 (MTSS VI, 102).

39. Ibid., 263 (MTSS VI, 113).

40. Gerhart, "Efficacy of Baptism," 1–44 (MTSS VI, 161–91). See

gued at length that such neglect of the sacrament was the inevitable result of the denial of its objective efficacy. He took it upon himself "with all due respect" to instruct his Presbyterian friends on the baptismal theology of Calvin and the Westminster Standards, suggesting in effect that they should be more true to their own confessional standards! Gerhart provided a number of quotations from Calvin affirming the saving efficacy of baptism, as well as a detailed interpretation of the section of the Westminster Confession of Faith dealing with baptism. Of particular significance is his reading of chapter 28.6: "The efficacy of baptism is not tied to that moment of time wherein it is administered; yet notwithstanding, by the right use of this ordinance, the grace promised is not only offered, but really exhibited and conferred by the Holy Ghost, to such (whether of age or infants) as that grace belongeth unto, according to the counsel of God's own will, in his appointed time." Gerhart contended that this referred to an efficacy that is immediate but extends throughout the recipient's lifetime: "The efficacy of the ordinance is indeed operative at the moment of time when it is administered; but not at that time exclusively . . . the efficacy of Baptism extends over the whole of life and terminates in the resurrection from the dead."[41]

Gerhart's interpretation here, however, fails to do full justice to the Confession's temporal conditioning of baptismal efficacy, and here it appears that Gerhart did not grasp some of the nuances of the classical Reformed tradition he referenced. Calvin's stated intent was to ascribe neither too much nor too little to the sacraments.[42] In this endeavor, he sought to account for three considerations—the objec-

---

Nichols, *Romanticism in American Theology*, 253–58.

41. Gerhart, "The Efficacy of Baptism," 21 (MTSS VI, 175).

42. See Calvin, *Institutes*, IV.14.17.

tive significance of baptism as "the laver of regeneration," the necessity of subjective reception by faith of sacramental grace that is offered, and the conditioning of sacramental efficacy by God's sovereign decree of predestination such that not all who receive the sacrament receive saving grace. Needless to say, this was quite a task, and what emerges is a subtle balancing of sacramental objectivity and subjectivity in which what is objectively offered must be subjectively received for baptism to be effectual. Calvin wrote:

> We must hold, therefore, that there is a mutual relation between faith and the sacraments, and hence, that the sacraments are effective through faith. Man's unworthiness does not detract anything from them, for they always retain their nature. Baptism is the laver of regeneration, although the whole world should be incredulous: (Tit. iii.5:) the Supper of Christ is the communication of his body and blood, (I Cor. x.16) although there were not a spark of faith in the world: but we do not perceive the grace which is offered to us; and although spiritual things always remain the same, yet we do not obtain their effect, nor perceive their value, unless we are cautious that our want of faith should not profane what God has consecrated to our salvation.[43]

This offer/reception model—baptism retains its objective character as an objective offer of divine grace and the grace offered in baptism can subsequently be appropriated or received by faith—implies what R. S. Wallace has helpfully termed a doctrine of "latent efficacy."[44] In other words,

43. Calvin, Commentary on Ezekiel 20:20.

44. Wallace, *Calvin's Doctrine of Word and Sacrament*, 185. On Calvin's "offer-reception" model, see Evans, "Calvin's Doctrine of the Lord's Supper," 8–9; "Really Exhibited and Conferred."

the promise and grace offered in baptism do not evaporate with the baptismal water and can be received by faith much later. Calvin wrote concerning his own experience:

> Now our opponents ask us what faith came to us during some years after our baptism . . . We therefore confess that for that time baptism benefited us not at all, inasmuch as the promise offered us in it—without which baptism is nothing—lay neglected . . . But we believe that the promise itself did not vanish. Rather, we consider that God through baptism promises us forgiveness of sins, and he will doubtless fulfill his promise for all believers. This promise was offered to us in baptism; therefore, let us embrace it by faith. Indeed, on account of our unfaithfulness it lay long buried from us; now, therefore, lest us receive it through faith.[45]

As Nevin's debate with Hodge over the Lord's Supper had demonstrated this balance of sacramental objectivity and subjectivity evident in Calvin and the Westminster Standards had been upset and many Americans Reformed Christians had effectively become Zwinglian subjectivists, but the argument can be made that especially with regard to baptism Mercersburg overcorrected and swung far in the opposite direction of sacramental objectivity.

The Lord's Supper, of course, was a matter of great importance to the Mercersburg theologians, in large measure because it was here that the saving relationship between Christ and the Christian came into especially clear focus, and one that provoked some heated polemical exchanges— most notably with the great Charles Hodge of Princeton Seminary. As Nevin put it, "Christianity is grounded in the living union of the believer with the person of Christ; and

45. Calvin, *Institutes*, IV.15.17.

this great fact is emphatically concentrated in the mystery of the Lord's Supper."[46]

Nevin's great 1846 work on the subject, *The Mystical Presence*, addressed what Nevin deemed a lamentable departure from the earlier Reformed teaching regarding the presence of Christ in the Supper. After presenting Calvin's views on the matter, Nevin critiqued what he called the "modern Puritan theory" of the sacrament, before proceeding to "scientific" and "biblical" defenses of the doctrine. "Puritanism" is a prominent foil in this and other of Nevin's writings; the term sometimes refers to the New England Calvinist tradition of Jonathan Edwards and his revivalist evangelical successors, and sometimes more generally to both evangelical New England Calvinism and the federal theology taught at Princeton Seminary. Both, according to Nevin, evinced a "rationalism" that had little room for the "mystery" of Christ's true presence in the sacrament. Nevin had been educated at schools associated with both traditions, and he admitted, "The hardest Puritan we have to do with always, is the one we carry, by birth and education, in our own bosom."[47]

Nevin's objections to New England Calvinism were substantial. Exponents of that tradition had reduced the Lord's Supper to an evocative psychological exercise, to little more than "a Fourth of July celebration" with no objective spiritual efficacy.[48] Nevin also opposed the view of union with Christ that underlay this theory, and he found the New England notion of a mere moral union of shared

46. Nevin, *Mystical Presence*, 51 (MTSS I, 40). The materials relating to the Nevin/Hodge debate over the Lord's Supper are collected in Nevin, *Mystical Presence and the Doctrine of the Reformed Church* (MTSS I), and Nevin and Hodge, *Coena Mystica* (MTSS II).

47. Nevin, "Puritanism and the Creed," 602.

48. Nevin, *Mystical Presence*, 117–26 (MTSS I, 103–11).

sentiment and purpose unsatisfying. The Reformed federal theology taught at Princeton was also found wanting by Nevin. While it made more room for a genuine spiritual efficacy of the sacrament involving the work of the Holy Spirit, it rejected the idea of a real union with Christ's incarnate humanity, and the Holy Spirit was really a sort of surrogate for an absent Christ. Union with Christ, according to Princeton theologians such as Charles Hodge, consisted of an extrinsic federal or "legal" union with Christ, by which the righteousness of Christ was imputed to the Christian, and a "spiritual" union that consisted in receiving the sanctifying work of the Holy Spirit. Furthermore, Nevin deemed this approach to the sacrament "abstract," for the Holy Spirit might or might not be at work in the Supper—the real determinant here was the eternal predestination of God, and thus there was no guarantee that the person receiving the sacrament was actually encountering grace.

Over against both New England and Princeton, Nevin insisted that in the Lord's Supper the Christian truly receives the incarnate humanity of Christ, and through that humanity the "whole Christ" by the power of the Holy Spirit. Only in this way, Nevin contended, can Christians receive the blessings of salvation because they are inseparable from Christ's person: "Our interests in Christ's merits and benefits can be based only upon a previous interest in his person . . . We partake of his merits only so far as we partake of his substance."[49] But this "substance" of Christ must not be understood, Nevin insisted, as material substance, as if the molecules of Christ's body and blood were physically present in the sacrament. Here Nevin was speaking self-consciously as a Reformed theologian in opposition to both Roman Catholic transubstantiation and Lutheran consubstantiation. Rather, it is a presence of Christ's very human

49. Ibid., 57 (MTSS I, 46).

life force, something more fundamental than the physical body and blood to which this life gave rise. As Nevin put it during his debate with Hodge, "Christ's flesh and blood are at hand, not in the bread and wine as such, but in the transaction; not materially or by mechanical contact in space, but *dynamically*, in the way of living substance and power; not for the outward man primarily and separately, as Luther contended, but for the *soul* (by no means to be confounded here with mere understanding or mind), as the central life of the whole person, so as to flow out from this to the *body* also as the true pabulum of immortality."[50]

In this Nevin was largely true to Calvin's intentions regarding the Supper (though he sometimes phrased matters in an idealist philosophical idiom that Calvin would not have recognized). There are, however, two areas where Nevin diverged from the Genevan Reformer. First, Nevin followed the German theologian Schleiermacher in arguing that there is a special communion with Christ in the Supper that is different in kind from the union that occurs when faith responds to the Word of God (Schleiermacher had wrongly argued that this was Calvin's position).[51] But according to Calvin, the sacraments "have the same office as the Word of God: to offer and set forth Christ to us, and in him the treasures of heavenly grace." Calvin went on, however, to explain that the sacraments are given because of human ignorance and weakness.[52] More true to Calvin's position is this striking statement by the sixteenth-century Scottish preacher Robert Bruce: "Why then is the Sacrament appointed? Not that you may get any new thing, but

50. Nevin, "Doctrine of the Reformed Church," 316 (MTSS I, 259).

51. See Nevin, *Mystical Presence*, 118, 182 (MTSS I, 104, 161); "Doctrine of the Reformed Church," 344, 358 (MTSS I, 281, 291).

52. Calvin, *Institutes*, IV.14.17. See also IV.14.3.

that you may get the same thing better than you had it in the Word."[53]

Second, Mercersburg diverged from Calvin and from the weight of the Reformed tradition over the issue of what Nevin termed the "metaphysical Calvinism" in which he had been reared. Calvin and the Westminster Confession taught that God chooses from all eternity the elect for salvation. In short, Calvin was a staunch predestinarian. Less well known is the fact that Martin Luther was as well. Here we think, for example, of Luther's critique of Erasmus in *The Bondage of the Will* and the programmatic distinction he makes between the hidden God of the decrees and the God revealed in Jesus Christ.[54] The later Lutheran tradition, however, softened the polarities in Luther's thought on this issue—a process that began with Luther's younger colleague Phillip Melanchthon. In the course of his debate over Lord's Supper with Charles Hodge of Princeton, Nevin concluded that Calvin's "abstract" doctrine of the decrees rendered the Incarnation, the atonement, and the sacraments a charade, and by 1848 Nevin had publicly and decisively broken with predestinarian Calvinism.[55]

Nevin's reasons for rejecting predestinarian Calvinism are worth exploring. With his historical, Christological, and sacramental interests, he was convinced that history is the theater in which real and meaningful human decisions are made, that God has genuinely stepped into history and accomplished salvation for the human race, and that that salvation is really made available to all in the sacraments and ministry of the church. He came to believe that genuine

53. Bruce, *Mystery of the Lord's Supper*, 64.

54. See Luther, *Bondage of the Will*.

55. See Nevin, "Doctrine of the Reformed Church," 372–73 (MTSS I, 301–2); "Hodge on the Ephesians," 46–83, 192–245 (MTSS VII, 62–125).

human freedom and the meaningfulness of the church's sacramental ministry were undercut by the notion that all events are simply the playing out of a divinely written script. Particular scorn was directed toward the doctrine of "limited atonement," the notion that Christ had died specifically for the elect rather than for the human race as a whole, and here we sense a tension between metaphysical Calvinism and Nevin's philosophical idealism, with its emphasis on unity and the whole over against particularity and the many. Furthermore, Schaff with his German Lutheran background was clearly of one mind with Nevin on these matters, and he would later write that a "theology constructed on the metaphysical doctrine of premundane decrees, or on the absolute sovereignty of God, is out of date."[56]

Thus it was that Nevin pitted the sacramental Calvin against the predestinarian Calvin. Pressed by Hodge on this and sensing a contradiction, Nevin argued that we must choose between the two!

> This [sacramental] doctrine, it is easy to see, de-
> rived no benefit from the connection in which it
> stood with the idea of predestination, as held by
> Calvin. It must be allowed, rather, that the sac-
> ramental interest and that of the decrees, in his
> system, are not free from some inward conflict,
> and that the one has a tendency continually to
> overthrow the other. Thus there is no doubt that
> in those sections of the Reformed Church where
> the doctrine of the decrees has been regarded as
> the main interest in theology, the original Cal-
> vinistic view of the sacraments has fallen more

56. Schaff, "Introduction," in Gerhart, *Institutes of the Christian Religion*, xiv.

and more into the shade, so as to be frequently of no authority whatever.[57]

But in rejecting a significant part of Calvin's legacy, were Nevin and Schaff departing from the Reformed tradition? Here the Mercersburg theologians appealed to what they took to be the distinctive tradition of the German Reformed Church as Melanchthonian on the decrees and Calvinistic on the sacraments—ideas that were being trumpeted in Germany at this time by August Ebrard and Heinrich Heppe.[58] This "Heppe Thesis," as it is sometimes called, was part of a broader historiographical discussion in Germany regarding how the Reformed tradition should be understood. More recent scholarship has tended to view the German Reformed tradition as more predestinarian than Ebrard and Heppe allowed, though conceding that the German Reformed emphasis has been more on the accomplishment and application of salvation in history than on eternal decrees.[59] But it is one thing to note the influence of Melanchthon; it is quite another, as Karl Barth ironically noted, to view him as the "Father of Reformed theology"![60] Nevertheless, the Heppe thesis did enable the Mercersburg theologians to carve out a meaningful past rooted in the German Reformed experience that distinguished them from the metaphysical Calvinists at Princeton.

57. Nevin, "Doctrine of the Reformed Church," 373 (MTSS I, 301–2).

58. See Wolff, "German Reformed Dogmatics." Philip Melanchthon (1497–1560) was a younger colleague of Martin Luther who softened Luther's teaching on predestination and the divine decrees.

59. See Weber, *Foundations of Dogmatics*, I:125; Bierma, *German Calvinism in the Confessional Age*.

60. Barth, "Foreword," in Heppe, *Reformed Dogmatics*, vii.

QUESTIONS

1. What two themes helped to shape the Mercersburg understanding of historical development?

2. What is the relationship between the "ideal" and the "actual" church?

3. How did the Mercersburg theologians answer the question of religious authority?

4. Why did the issue of baptismal efficacy pose a special problem for Nevin?

5. How did the sacraments cause the Mercersburg theologians to break decisively with Calvin's predestinarianism?

6

MINISTRY, WORSHIP, AND LITURGY

THIS DISTINCTIVE MERCERSBURG SOTERIOLOGY and ecclesiology discussed in the preceding chapters expressed itself
in high views of ministry, worship, and liturgy. As it happened, issues involving the Christian ministry presented
themselves with urgency first, and so we will examine these
developments in that order.

THE MINISTRY OF THE CHURCH

Here we will recall that the visibility of the church was crucial for Mercersburg; the ideal must actualize itself in history, in an actual and visible church. Thus the visible structure
of the church as it was reflected in the ordained ministry
was of vital importance. And yet the visible church as Nevin and Schaff experienced it in America was chaotic and

divided almost beyond imagination. Nevin had excoriated this situation in essays such as "The Sect System" (1848), but that diagnosis in turn raised the question of where the true church was to be found and what the principles of that ecclesial identity might be. And so Nevin studied the early church for insight and help. While a wide variety of differences between Catholicism and Protestantism emerged in these explorations, issues involving the ministry seem to have been crucial to Nevin's thinking during this period, and it is worthwhile to examine how Nevin's thinking unfolded.

Immediately, however, we are confronted with a problem. Nevin was the primary ecclesiological theoretician among the Mercersburg theologians, and yet his pronouncements on the ministry are to some degree conflicted and even contradictory. Recall that Nevin's period of "dizziness" from 1851 to 1854 reflected, in reality, a serious loss of ecclesiological equilibrium. Nevin's studies of the early church resulted in a serious questioning of the legitimacy of Protestantism over against the claims of Rome and the Papacy. Such was the seriousness of this "church question" that Nevin for a time considered submission to the Pope. Thus care must be taken to read these materials in context, for some of what Nevin writes this period stands in tension with what he had written previously and with what he would subsequently express.

Nevin's 1851–52 series of articles titled "Early Christianity" was a sustained polemic against the popular "Apostasy Theory" in both its reigning Protestant forms. Puritanism sought to go back behind medieval and early Catholicism to recover the New Testament church, and Anglicanism wanting to recover the church of the first four centuries of the Christian movement before the excesses of the Papacy emerged. But such efforts to bypass the Catholic past are impossible; there is no Protestant past to be recovered, for Christianity from the second century onward was recognizeably "Catholic." The early church was sacramental and insisted on reading the Bible in light of the tradition of the church rather than in terms of *sola Scriptura*. Puritan Protestantism focuses on justification by faith, while the early church made the doctrine of the Incarnation central. A penitential system was evident early on, with the confession of sin, penance, and absolution. Furthermore, the early church venerated relics of saints and championed asceticism in the form of voluntary poverty, celibacy, and monasticism. All this disquieted Nevin.

But it was in the area of the ministry that the differences were perhaps most stark. Simply put, Nevin came to believe that the early church's conception of ministry was profoundly hierarchical (in contrast to the ecclesiastical democracy championed by many Protestants), and that this hierarchical structure of bishops in apostolic succession going back to the apostles was seen as the source of the church's power and ministry: "Hence the stress laid on the hierarchy, as the bond, not from below but from above, of that glorious *sacramentum unitatis* on which is felt to hand the virtue and value of all grace in the church besides."[1] And equally shocking to Protestants, communion with the bishop of Rome as the successor of Peter was assumed.

Given this remarkable discontinuity between Protestantism and early Christianity, how might Protestantism be sustained as a legitimate form of Christianity? When he wrote these articles on "Early Christianity," Nevin still believed that Schaff's theory of historical development might vindicate both Catholicism and Protestantism as legitimate and successive moments in church history. But

1. Nevin, "Early Christianity," 541 (*Catholic and Reformed*, 235).

that optimism soon dissipated as Nevin studied the third-century North African bishop Cyprian of Carthage (c. 200–258). In his mid-third century context, Cyprian was a crucial figure defending the hierarchical prerogatives of bishops and the sacramental nature of the church. According to Cyprian, there is "no salvation outside the church," and schism is the equivalent of heresy. Nevin took pains to present Cyprian as a figure of remarkable piety and "the complete ideal of a true Christian bishop," but he scarcely could have found a figure to contrast more starkly with nineteenth-century Protestantism.[2]

Nevin highlights a number of Cyprianic principles. Once again, the top-down, hierarchical principle of the ministry is noted:

> The church pyramid, in his view, started from its own summit, not from its base. The only true order of its constitution, and so of the derivation of its functions and powers, was: Christ first, the head of the universal organism; then the Apostolate continued by regular succession in the Episcopate; then the Ministry in its lower orders and finally the body of the people held in connection with the head through the medium of this hierarchy, which is thus Divinely ordained to be the one only channel of all descending communications of life and grace.[3]

In addition, the episcopacy is the foundation of the unity of the Church, but the episcopacy itself must have a principle of unity and it finds this in the Bishop of Rome. While the episcopacy in Cyprian's time was marked by the collegial approach that still exists in Eastern Orthodoxy (in contrast to the later Papal system in the West),

2. Nevin, "Cyprian," 264.

3. Ibid., 361.

it nevertheless looked to the Bishop of Rome as the focal point of unity. Nevin wrote: "Such an actual primacy and real centre of unity for the universal Episcopal college, there can be no reasonable question or doubt, Cyprian habitually saw and acknowledged in the pontificate of the Bishop of Rome; which was regarded as flowing with such right of priority, from the place originally assigned to Peter by our Blessed Lord himself in the joint commission of the Apostles."[4]

As we noted above, there is a marked shift in tone from "Early Christianity" to "Cyprian." In the earlier articles Nevin focused his criticism primarily on New England "Puritanism" and he held out hope that Schaff's theory of development would vindicate Protestantism. By the time his articles on Cyprian appeared, however, Nevin seemed convinced that the problem was not just Puritanism but Protestantism in general. As Nevin put it,

> Protestantism, it is plain, involves an entire departure from the theory or scheme of Cyprian here, not simply as it may reject this or that form of ecclesiastical polity, this or that ecclesiastical usage, but as it refuses to see in the church the actual presence of the Christian salvation under the same outwardly real and objective view . . . So far as Puritanism is concerned, the difference is immediately palpable . . . But the Puritan system in this case is not alone . . . The difference is with Protestantism as a whole. It is not to be disguised, that this rests upon a doctrine of the church, which is broadly at variance with the doctrine of Cyprian.[5]

4. Ibid., 367.
5. Ibid., 421–22.

While Nevin mentions the theory of historical development in this context as the only hope for vindicating Protestantism, he declines to endorse it: "We are shut up then of course, so far as we have any faith in Protestantism, to the theory of historical development, as the only possible way of setting it in living union with the Divine fact of early Christianity . . . If it be asked now, what precise construction we propose to apply to the subject, we have only to say that we have none to offer whatsoever . . . We have no theory to assert or uphold. We offer no speculation."[6]

By 1854, however, Nevin had recovered a measure of his theological and emotional equilibrium. In November of that year he preached a sermon based on Ephesians 4:8–16 on the occasion of the installation of his successor, B. C. Wolff, at Mercersburg. In it, earlier themes are again raised but with some moderation and modification: in contrast to American democratic impulses, the ministry precedes the church and derives its authorization from the Apostles rather than the body of believers. In keeping with this, the basic impulse continues to be hierarchical. Nevin also embraces the term "bishop" as expressive of this hierarchy, but he is careful not to insist on one particular form of the office. Rather, the issue is one of real pastoral care, responsibility, and authority over the church. Nevin writes: "The question is not of the episcopal office in some special given form; but of the office in its broad New Testament sense, as involving the idea of a real pastoral jurisdiction over the Church, representing in it immediately the authority of Jesus Christ, and deriving its force from the sovereignty of heaven and earth to which he has been advanced by his resurrection from the dead."[7]

---

6. Ibid., 562–63.

7. Nevin, "The Christian Ministry," 80 (MTSS VII, 47).

Likewise, Nevin continued to insist on some tangible form of historical succession from the Apostles to the present. Continuity with Christ and the historical church involves succession, and "the succession, to be valid, must be kept up in some way within the bosom of the institution itself."[8] But what this "succession" might look like exactly, Nevin does not explain, and we are left to surmise that Nevin the Protestant theologian finally realized that Protestant lines of succession through the Reformation are not to be rejected out of hand.

In retrospect, while Nevin's existential anxiety over the "church question" is palpable during this period, his depiction of the relationship of Protestantism/Puritanism and Catholicism in this period is problematic and occasionally ham-fisted. Catholicism is generally presented in a positive light, and Protestantism in more negative tones, and all the while Nevin opines that he is simply presenting incontrovertible historical facts! He seems to have viewed Protestantism and Catholicism as discrete and completely dissimilar impulses driven by different "ideas" of the church, but the reality is more complicated. For example, twentieth-century scholarship has uncovered some profound links between medieval Catholic piety and the Puritans that Nevin despised.[9] In addition, Nevin's version of "Catholicism" is heavily Latin and Western in orientation, and not surprisingly the discussion is dominated by questions of institutional continuity and structure. J. H. Nichols aptly notes Nevin's preference for legal and governmental metaphors in this context: "It is significant that Nevin uses political analogies almost exclusively. The role of the minister is put in terms of government, of supervision, of domination. The church is conceived as a kind of sacred state

8. Ibid., 82 (MTSS VII, 48).

9. See, e.g., Hambrick-Stowe, *Practice of Piety*, 25–39.

. . . The unity and continuity described here seem purely institutional and legal. There is no word of unity of apostolic faith or love or service, or how variously they are related to administrative unity. There is no criterion of apostolicity save institutional continuity."[10] But precisely here there is an irony. For all of Nevin's arguments favoring the inward and the concrete over against the external, mechanical, and abstract, his discussions of the church during this period seem favor the latter.[11] Finally, Nevin's relentless emphasis on hierarchy and top-down structure will be tiresome to many.

Thus far we have discussed ministerial functions only in passing. Here we should expect a Christological starting point, and Nevin finds it in the *munus triplex*, or "threefold office" of prophet, priest, and king, that was utilized by Calvin and then popularized in the Reformed tradition. In Protestant theology the work of Christ has generally been presented in terms of two approaches—the threefold office and the humiliation/exaltation schemes. In his 1851 theological lectures (the closest thing we have to comprehensive dogmatics by Nevin), Nevin utilizes the threefold-office approach but includes the stages of humiliation and exaltation under the priestly office.[12] The prominence of the threefold office is not accidental, for Nevin regarded it as required by the human condition: "The work of redemption requires this triplicity of offices, because there is a three-fold necessity for it in the human nature. Man was ignorant, guilty and polluted. The prophetical office was required to dispel

---

10. Nichols, *Romanticism in American Theology*, 279.

11. This irony has been noted by Littlejohn, "Search for Visible Catholicity," 131.

12. See Erb, *Nevin's Theology*, 247–80.

the cloud of ignorance, the priestly to atone for our guilt, and the kingly to redeem us from our pollution."[13]

Nevin also insists that by virtue of the church's union with Christ, these functions continue to be exercised in the church. Thus, the teachings of the church "constitute the prophetical office of Christ as administered through the Church" and "the ministry of the Church is the ministry of Christ."[14] Likewise, the priestly functions of offering sacrifices and interceding continue in the church. In significant contrast to the weight of Protestant tradition, Nevin insists that ministers should be regarded as "priests" whose sacerdotal activities of offering the sacrifice of the Lord's Supper, proclaiming absolution for sins, and interceding for the people are real and effectual. Nevin contended,

> We must perceive how unsatisfactory and how wrong it is to make the ordinances of the Church merely declaratory, commemorative, or symbolical. The acts of the Church must be regarded as living acts. The power of Christ's intercession must be regarded as something present in the Church . . . There is no new sacrifice in the Lord's Supper, but there is present the power of that one made on the cross . . . The true view is that this one sacrifice is always new in the Church, of the same force and power as if it were actually present at the time. The sacrifice is not repeated, but it perpetuates itself.[15]

And finally, the kingly office of Christ is also perpetuated in the church. Again, Nevin writes: "If the kingship of Christ is something that carries itself forward in the world, it must be through the Church as a medium. The authority

13. Erb, *Nevin's Theology*, 248.

14. Ibid., 251.

15. Ibid., 255–56.

which the Church exercises in performing the kingly function depends upon the presence of Christ in the Church. The Church is the body of Christ, and the members are participants of His life, and consequently of His office."[16]

It is precisely here, however, that we sense significant tension between the organic, Christological Nevin and the hierarchical, legal, and extrinsic Nevin. Note that here the kingly functions of the church are rooted in the organic union of the church as a whole with the person of Christ, and thereby with his threefold office. In this context we find no mention of mechanical apostolic succession as the guarantor of the office, and it seems that, whether he fully realized it or not, Nevin was caught between his Christology and his desire to impose some sort of theological order on the sectarian chaos of his day.

But where does the emphasis lie? It is not accidental that Nevin's discussion of the priestly office of Christ and its implications for the ministry of the church is the most extensive of the three. Nevin clearly believed that the distinctively priestly function of the ministry had been slighted in the American context, and that this was due in large measure to a democratizing and leveling impulse that emphasized the "priesthood of all believers" instead. The cost of this corrective for Mercersburg, however, was substantial. First, it is precisely here that the tension between Mercersburg and the weight of the Reformed tradition was greatest. There were well-considered reasons why Reformed theologians hesitated to call ministers "priests," and the Lord's Table an "altar." Moreover, that tradition also emphasized the priority of the Word in the life of the church rather than the sacraments. The friction between the sacerdotal shape of ministry proposed by Nevin and the Reformed tradition from Calvin onward was real. Second, the extensive and

16. Ibid., 280.

divisive opposition to Mercersburg-inspired liturgical developments largely centered on these issues, and it is to that story that we now turn.

WORSHIP AND LITURGY

The connection between theology and worship was explicit for the Mercersburg theologians. Liturgical scholar Howard Hageman has contended, with perhaps a bit of exaggeration, that "it was at Mercersburg that there was worked out, often in the heat of battle, for the first time in the Reformed churches what could be called a theology of the liturgy."[17] Here we recall the periodization of the Mercersburg movement proposed by E. V. Gerhart, in which the third stage (1858–1866) was the liturgical as Nevin's theology and Philip Schaff's remarkable knowledge of liturgical history—unparalleled in the United States at that time—were brought to bear on the issue.

The theology informing the liturgical contributions of the German Reformed Church in the 1850s and 1860s should be apparent from the material above. Liturgical expression shaped by Mercersburg sensibilities regarding the Incarnation and Christ's living presence in the church would give voice to a catholicity embracing the whole of church history rather than simply focusing on the Reformation and post-Reformation Protestant tradition of worship. It would reflect the centrality of the sacraments and the sacramental in the life of the church as real means of grace. And finally, it would highlight the priestly aspects of ministry and worship, as well as a hierarchical sensibility regarding the structure and organization of the church.

The "Liturgical Movement," as Nevin called it, in the German Reformed Church has been ably and exhaustively

17. Hageman, *Pulpit and Table*, 92.

chronicled by Jack M. Maxwell, but a brief summary is in order here.[18] The old Palatinate liturgy that the German Reformed had brought over from Germany in the early eighteenth century had fallen into disuse; in fact, copies of it were difficult to find by the early nineteenth century, and worship in the German Reformed Church was increasingly shaped by the prevailing low-church, non-liturgical sensibilities. There were a number of efforts to provide ministers with worship resources and helps—collections of forms for the celebration of marriages, baptisms, the Lord's Supper, ordination, and so forth—most notably the pulpit book compiled by Nevin's predecessor at Mercersburg, Lewis Mayer, and first published in 1837.[19] But these did not meet with broad acceptance, and in 1849 the Eastern Synod meeting in Norristown, Pennsylvania, endorsed the use of liturgical forms in worship and appointed a "Liturgical Committee" of eminent denominational leaders, including Nevin as chair, Schaff, Henry Harbaugh, B. C. Wolff, J. H. A. Bomberger, and J. F. Berg, to produce a new liturgy for the church. The Synod envisioned that the resulting product would be distinctly Protestant and draw on Reformation-era and later liturgies—no mention was made of liturgies from the early church. Ironically, Bomberger would later emerge as the most determined opponent of the Mercersburg-inspired liturgy.

The committee, now chaired by Schaff, presented a preliminary report to the Eastern Synod at Baltimore in 1852, and this report signaled a significant change of direction. J. H. Nichols identifies three aspects of this report

18. Maxwell, *Worship and Reformed Theology*. Nevin, *Vindication of the Revised Liturgy*, 313–403 is a lively, albeit not disinterested, source for this history.

19. *Liturgy for the Use of the Congregations of the German Reformed Church*.

as particularly significant.[20] First, the committee recommended that the historical scope be expanded such that "the liturgical worship of the Primitive Church" as reflected in "the oldest ecclesiastical writings, and the liturgies of the Greek and Latin Churches of the third and fourth centuries, ought to be made . . . the general basis of the proposed Liturgy," adding that "special reference ought to be had to the old Palatinate and other Reformed liturgies of the sixteenth century."[21] Clearly, what the committee majority envisioned was a liturgy that was both catholic and Reformed. Second, the committee wanted to produce a "people's liturgy" similar to the Anglican *Book of Common Prayer*, in which the laity could follow along and respond audibly at appropriate points in the service. There were also sacramental implications entailed in this shift, for it also signaled a transferal of the liturgical center of gravity from the preached word to the Lord's Supper—Nevin, in fact, framed the contrast here as between "two orders of worship (pulpit liturgy and altar liturgy)."[22] And finally, the committee wanted to incorporate the celebration of the feasts of the church year into its liturgy. All this effort was distinctive in the American context and reflected the Mercersburg theological sensibility.

In 1857 the Liturgical Committee presented its "Provisional Liturgy" to the German Reformed Church for optional use in its congregations. Further revisions by the same Liturgical Committee resulted in *An Order of Worship for the Reformed Church*, published in 1866, but by this time a full-scale liturgical controversy was roiling the church. The impetus for liturgical reform came from the Eastern Synod of the German Reformed Church centered in Pennsylvania where, of course, the influence of the Mercersburg

20. Nichols, *Romanticism in American Theology*, 296–98.

21. Quoted in Nevin, *Vindication of the Revised Liturgy*, 327.

22. Nevin, *Vindication of the Revised Liturgy*, 343.

theologians was greater, while the less-numerous Western Synod was more resistant to these liturgical initiatives. More importantly, a member of the Liturgical Committee, J. H. A. Bomberger, emerged as a decided opponent of what he derided as the "ritualism" of Mercersburg.[23] By the late 1870s, however, a majority of the German Reformed Church was tired of the controversy. A "Peace Commission" with membership reflecting the various parties in the debate was established, and in 1881 it recommended the production of a new liturgical resource. The *Directory of Worship*, a modest revision of the 1866 *Order of Worship* in which some language offensive to the anti-Mercersburg wing of the church was removed, was published in 1884, and by the 1890s the church had clearly decided that a *laissez faire* approach to worship was the best policy for maintaining denominational tranquility.[24] The result was that the Mercersburg wing of the church was free to implement its theology liturgically, but not to carry the church as a whole along with it.

What were the major friction points in this liturgical controversy? Three general areas may be noted. The first was the notion of liturgy itself. Nevin was convinced on solid historical grounds that Christian worship from the beginning had involved the use of set forms with extensive congregational participation, and he believed, furthermore, that liturgical worship was of a piece with the whole Mercersburg theological program: "A theology that is truly Christocentric, must follow the Creed, must be objective, must be historical; with this must be churchly; and with this again, must be sacramental and liturgical."[25] But this emphasis created tension with the Reformed tradition—not so

23. See Bomberger, *Reformed, Not Ritualistic*.

24. See Maxwell, *Worship and Reformed Theology*, 323–34.

25. Nevin, *Vindication of the Revised Liturgy*, 381.

much because of the use of liturgy *per se* (Calvin's Geneva and Strasbourg liturgies show him to have been a capable liturgist), but rather with how it was justified. The magisterial Reformation had sought to navigate the nexus of *sola Scriptura* and worship by means of a "regulative principle of worship." Lutherans and Anglicans affirmed a negative warrant: it is permissible to worship in ways that are not expressly forbidden by Scripture. The Reformed, however, adopted a more stringent positive warrant: only that which is expressly commanded in Scripture may be done in worship. Consistent with his rejection of *sola Scriptura*, Nevin found both of these approaches to be unnecessarily legalistic: "That view by which rites are limited positively and negatively is narrow and Judaistical."[26]

Antipathy to liturgy often coalesced around the issue of "free prayer"—the freedom of the minister and other members of the congregation to compose their own prayers in the context of worship. Few things were more symbolic of the democratizing trends in American Christianity, and Mercersburg's more prescriptive approach was controversial and disturbing to many. The Mercersburg suspicion of free prayer was rooted, first of all, in the sense that the average minister was not capable of consistently composing prayers of beauty and substance that would edify the congregation. Moreover, free prayer was generally regarded as an exercise by the individual minister rather than an act involving the congregation. Nevin wrote:

> Public worship ought to be liturgical, whether as free or in the use of forms. Most men view free prayer as the product of separate thinking and reflection of the minister. But in such a form it is always defective and unliturgical. Prayer, to be as it should be, must be liturgical, must bear the

26. Erb, *Nevin's Theology*, 459.

> general religious life of the congregation, must
> be the representation of a general religious life.
> When we view it in this light we will find but few
> free liturgical prayers. We meet with many good
> sermons before we meet a single good prayer in
> this sense.[27]

Another point of tension was the form for the service of ministerial ordination. Nevin and the Liturgical Committee were convinced that ordination by the laying on of hands is "the channel of supernatural official endowment for the work of the ministry."[28] This high view of the ministry was, of course, a conviction Mercersburg shared with other "catholicizing" movements of the period, such as the Oxford Movement in England and High-Church Confessional Lutheranism in Germany, for whom the assertion of the status and prerogatives of the ministry over against both democratizing impulses and efforts to control the church by the state was a vital element of their "let the church be the church" programs.[29] Nevertheless, this high view of ordination as expressed in the Mercersburg-inspired liturgies provoked considerable opposition. A formidable expression of such opposition came, interestingly enough, from the German mediating theologian I. A. Dorner, who responded to Nevin's *Vindication of the Revised Liturgy* by suggesting that Nevin had made ordination a "sacrament," that "these views of Ordination far transcend the limits of evangelical theology, and must lead to the hierarchical system," and that it involves a form of "magic."[30]

27. Ibid., 414.

28. Nevin, *Vindication of the Revised Liturgy*, 392.

29. See Conser, *Church and Confession*; Nichols, *Romanticism in American Theology*, 260.

30. Dorner, *The Liturgical Conflict*, 29–30.

Finally, there were objections having to do with how the Mercersburg liturgies emphasized the priestly work of ministry. Charges of "sacerdotalism" were frequent and focused especially on the liturgies of confession and absolution and the Lord's Supper. With regard to the former, we will recall Nevin's insistence that "the absolution of the Church is not a mere declarative act, but that she comprehends the medium for the communication of the forgiveness of sins."[31] In other words, the absolution pronounced was understood to be effectual, and thus a more momentous affair than the "assurance of pardon" familiar to Presbyterians. Likewise, the liturgy of the Lord's Supper was replete with "altar" and "sacrifice" language, and the structure of the service clearly shifted the center of gravity from sermon to sacrament. Some of this, of course, stood in considerable tension with the classical Reformed tradition from the sixteenth century onward, and not surprisingly the compromise 1884 *Directory of Worship* allowed more room for free prayer in the services of the church; the language of ordination was modified, and the sacerdotal language toned down.[32]

As we noted earlier in this chapter, proponents of the Mercersburg theology were able to instill Mercersburg theological sensibilities in much of the Eastern Synod of the German Reformed Church, but they was less successful in convincing the denomination as a whole. Furthermore, the Mercersburg Theology itself became a bone of contention between supporters of Mercersburg and those who viewed it as an incipient betrayal of the Reformation. Ironically perhaps, a theology that placed the unity and catholicity of the church as the body of Christ at its center was, particularly

31. Erb, *Nevin's Theology*, 367.

32. On these changes, see Maxwell, *Worship and Reformed Theology*, 326–30.

during the extended liturgical controversy, an occasion for discord and disunity. One can speculate as to how much of that discord was necessary.

The Mercersburg theologians were, of course, theologians! They were able to discern implications and connect the dots in ways that the average congregant and even many church leaders were not. But with this perhaps came a penchant for insisting on too much, and here their philosophical idealism likely was an impediment. If the many facets of church life are but the working out of a particular "idea of the church," then virtually everything can be seen as essential. But was it wise, for example, to insist on excluding free prayer from services? Was it prudent to throw prescribed "altar" and "sacrifice" language in the faces of those who were sure to be offended by it? In short, could the Mercersburgers (and Nevin in particular) have accomplished more in their context had they been more diplomatic? Such questions are difficult to answer, but there are likely some practical lessons here for theologians and liturgical reformers today.

QUESTIONS

1. How did his study of the ministry in the early church cause Nevin to question the legitimacy of Protestantism?

2. What tensions are evident in Nevin's theology of the Christian ministry?

3. In what ways does Nevin emphasize the "priestly" aspects of ministry?

4. What points of disagreement contributed to the liturgical conflict in the German Reformed Church?

Epilogue

THE CONTINUING RELEVANCE OF MERCERSBURG

DOES A THEOLOGICAL MOVEMENT in a small immigrant denomination that flourished for about two decades in mid-nineteenth century America have continuing relevance over a century and a half later? The quiet persistence of scholarly interest in Mercersburg since the 1950s, and especially the more recent efforts to make key Mercersburg texts available once again for the twenty-first century suggest that the theology that emerged from a small hamlet in south-central Pennsylvania so long ago continues to resonate.

Reasons for this continued interest are not difficult to find. The Mercersburg Theology provides a decided alternative to both moralistic liberalism and to the ahistoricism and excessive subjectivity of evangelicalism. Mercersburg also reminds us of the centrality of Christology for the Christian faith. Salvation, for Mercersburg, is "in Christ" and not simply on the basis of what Christ has done, and here we see a close, indeed integral, connection between Christ's person and work. Mercersburg also represents a salutary recovery of the ontological—over against superficial moralisms (evident on both the left and the right that seem to think that the human problem can be solved with either more education about "diversity" or by instilling proper beliefs about right and wrong), Mercersburg recognized that humanity is diseased and needs to be set free from its bondage to sin and death. It held that a new and supernatural principle of human existence has been introduced with the Incarnation. Mercersburg also represents a recovery of ecclesiology.

Over against a liberalism that sometimes views the church as little more than a collection of resources that may assist social improvement efforts, and an evangelicalism that views the church as a helpful but less-than-essential aid to the piety of individual Christians, Mercersburg took the church with deadly seriousness. The church is nothing less than the sphere of divine salvation on earth. And finally, Mercersburg just might offer resources that will help contemporary Christians transcend the persistent divides between orthodox and progressive expressions of Christianity, and between those who are more "Catholic" and more "evangelical."

After several decades of studying and reflecting on the Mercersburg theology, however, I sense that the continuing relevance of Mercersburg hinges on the answers to three broad questions. First, is the Mercersburg theology so tied to a particular nineteenth-century intellectual context that the translation of its key themes and ideas to our context is impossible? Second, does the Mercersburg Theology have something significant to contribute to contemporary theological discussions? And finally, is Mercersburg so tied to a hierarchical view of social reality far out of step with contemporary sensibilities that it simply will not be heard by many today?

INTELLECTUAL CONTEXT

At various points we have seen the influence of German idealism on the Mercersburg theologians. To be sure, they operated with an idealist ontology—reality as we experience it is the ideal struggling to actualize itself—and the dialectical teleology of Hegel and Schelling has been evident at key points in the Mercersburg approach to history. And so a question is posed: Is the Mercersburg theology so tied to nineteenth-century German speculative idealism that it cannot speak with any real power to a quite different philosophical context? Or, to phrase the matter differently, were the Mercersburg thinkers idealist theologians *simpliciter*, or are they better seen as Protestant theologians with deep biblical, patristic, and Reformation roots who found the apparatus of German idealism useful as an idiom for expressing certain concerns but were willing to diverge from it where necessary? This is a serious question, for nineteenth-century German speculative idealism represents a totalizing impulse that stands in considerable tension with contemporary concerns for diversity. Moreover, the naïve metanarrative of progress generated by such *bagatelle* Hegelianism is unappealing to many today (excepting, perhaps, American politicians who opine about the importance of being "on the right side of history").

Test cases involving Christology and history—two central elements of the Mercersburg Theology—suggest that the Mercersburg theologians are, on balance, better viewed in the latter terms. Here we will recall Nevin's engagement with the question of the rationale for the Incarnation that we discussed in Chapter Four above. An implication of the idealist Christology was that the Incarnation would have occurred even apart from the fall of the human race into sin. Nevin wrote lengthy reviews of arguments on this issue pro and con without taking a final position on the matter, and some of Nevin's later writings on Christology are notable for their presentation in a more biblical than philosophical idiom.[1] Likewise, as we saw in Chapter Five, it appears that Nevin, while holding on to the notion of organic historical change, relinquished the more dialectical and Hegelian view of historical progress in the 1850s. As Nevin discovered, the history of the church is too convoluted and complicated to be framed in terms of a facile narrative of inexorable progress. In retrospect, the Mercersburg use of the dialectical Hegelian historiography, especially early on, would seem to be an unhappy instance of superimposing an essentially secular view of progress upon church history. Furthermore, it was not essential to the Mercersburg movement.

At the same time, insofar as it stands in the "great tradition" of Christian Platonism, the generally idealist orientation of Mercersburg may well be an asset in our contemporary context. More recent theologians as diverse as the Roman Catholic *nouvelle théologie* of Henri de Lubac and Yves Congar, John Milbank (Anglican), and Hans Boersma (Dutch Reformed) have responded to the modern disenchantment and desacralization of the cosmos and the resulting nihilism and social atomism by seeking to recover great Platonic Christian themes of analogy, participation, sacramentality, and ecclesiology.[2] The points of contact

---

1. See, e.g., Nevin, "Jesus and the Resurrection."

2. Affinities of Mercersburg and the *nouvelle théologie* are

between such programs and the Mercersburg Theology are substantial and worthy of further exploration. All this suggests that the philosophical orientation of Mercersburg is no final impediment to contemporary relevance.

RELEVANCE TO CONTEMPORARY THEOLOGY

The preceding paragraph has already begun to address the question of the relevance of Mercersburg for contemporary theology. In fact, the Mercersburg Theology was prescient in anticipating certain twentieth and twenty-first century theological interests. For example, in a 2009 article I noted some remarkable convergences between the theologies of John W. Nevin and the Scottish theologian Thomas F. Torrance having to do with theological method, the incarnate humanity of Christ, and salvation as participation in Christ.[3]

More to the point, however, is the question of whether Mercersburg can make a decided positive contribution to contemporary discussion. I believe it can.[4] In recent years there has been an upsurge of interest in the notion of "participation in Christ" evident in Anglican, Lutheran, Methodist, and Reformed circles. For example, in 2008 I argued, drawing on insights from Calvin, Mercersburg, and Torrance, that both the forensic and the transformatory elements of salvation can be fruitfully articulated in terms of "participation" in Christ, and that from such thinking flows a renewed ecclesiology which recognizes that "the

---

explored in Littlejohn, *Mercersburg Theology and the Quest for Reformed Catholicity*, 147–69. See also Boersma, *Heavenly Participation*.

3. See Evans, "Twin Sons of Different Mothers."

4. The argument in this section was first presented in Evans, "The Mercersburg Christology and Reformed *Ressourcement*," 400–403.

pilgrimage of the individual Christian is ineluctably connected with the pilgrimages of other Christians through union together with the life of Christ."[5] From a Lutheran perspective, the notion of participation in Christ has been fruitfully explored by the Finnish school of Luther interpretation and by Robert Jensen.[6] Calvin's participationist theology of union with Christ has been insightfully examined at length by Todd Billings and Julie Canlis.[7] As we noted above, Hans Boersma, a Reformed theologian with a deep interest in the Roman Catholic *Nouvelle Théologie*, has called for a return to the participationist "Platonist-Christian synthesis" of the "great tradition" that is, at its best, both Trinitarian and Christocentric.[8] John Milbank and others connected with the Radical Orthodoxy movement have foregrounded the theme of participation.[9] Finally, in another recent volume Roger Owens has explored a variety of participationist approaches to Christology and ecclesiology, and has argued that a participationist framework is vital for an ecclesiology that does justice to the visibleness, physicality, and practices of the church.[10]

These writers are not on the same page with respect to the nature and implications of participationist views of salvation and ecclesiology. There are differences over the role of philosophical ontology, the role of the person of Christ, and the nature of participation itself. This is not surprising, in that the broader current interest in participation is coming from at least three quarters—from Radical Orthodoxy

5. Evans, *Imputation and Impartation*, 266.

6. See, e.g., Braaten and Jensen, eds., *Union with Christ*.

7. See Billings, *Calvin, Participation, and the Gift*; Canlis, *Calvin's Ladder*.

8. See Boersma, *Heavenly Participation*.

9. See, e.g., Milbank et al, "Suspending the Material."

10. Owens, *The Shape of Participation*.

with its more Neoplatonic, creationally focused program, from those concerned to transcend the forensic/spiritual dualism evident in later Reformed views of salvation, and from those who are responding to a set of problems regarding the importance and coherence of human action arising from Karl Barth's objectivism and actualism. Rather, for a variety of reasons the discussion of participation has reached critical mass, and the point here is that Mercersburg anticipated some of this discussion in its nineteenth-century context and should legitimately be included in the contemporary discussion.

We may further locate Mercersburg in the current context by comparing it with two other current options— Radical Orthodoxy (RO) and Karl Barth. As Roger Owens rightly notes, RO thinker John Milbank "has done more than anyone to bring the theological topic of participation back onto the theological scene."[11] Milbank and his RO colleagues have argued at length that in medieval nominalism created reality was uncoupled from its transcendent foundation in God. Unable to sustain value and significance on its own, reality was "flattened" and western culture slouched toward nihilism. Drawing on Neoplatonism, they propose a participationist ontology in which created reality is "suspended" from the divine, and the Incarnation is understood as the preeminent manifestation of this participatory ontology. But here a problem emerges—the Incarnation for RO seems to be little more than an example or lesson in service to a creational ontology rather than the classical Christian tradition's decisive act of redemption, reconciliation, and recreation.[12] In short, RO is participa-

11. Ibid., 133.

12. Quite a variety of criticisms along this line have been voiced. See, e.g., Smith, "Will the Real Plato Please Stand Up?," 61–72; Boersma, *Heavenly Participation*, 20; Owens, *Shape of Participation*, 137.

tionist but not especially Christocentric. And not surprisingly, this combination of Platonizing participation focused on the divine upholding of creation coupled with a lack of a really decisive Christology then issues in an undeveloped ecclesiology.[13]

Karl Barth develops the theme of solidarity with Christ in discussions of election and vocation.[14] These two contexts correspond to the two forms of Barthian "participation" in Christ helpfully explicated by Adam Neder. First, Jesus Christ is the electing God as well as the representative elect and reprobate human being who accomplishes salvation for all and absorbs the divine penalty for sin. Thus creation and humanity comprehensively considered must be understood in relation to Jesus Christ, and there is a "de jure" or "objective" participation of all in Christ.[15] Key here is Barth's "objectivism," in which Christ not only fulfilled the divine initiative toward sinful humanity, but also fulfills the human requirement of response in faith and obedience.

Second, there is what Neder terms a "de facto" or "subjective" participation in Christ, which Barth develops especially in the context of divine calling. Here "union with Christ" is framed in actualistic terms where the focus is on event, decision, and personal confrontation and encounter, and in speaking of this relationship Barth clearly prefers the term "fellowship" to "union."[16] In this relationship of encounter Christ calls the Christian through the Holy Spirit and the Christian responds with faith and obedience.[17] In short, the Christian's "union with Christ" consists in this

13. Owens, *Shape of Participation*, 144, speaks of Milbank's "absent ecclesiology."

14. See Barth, *Church Dogmatics*, II/2, 3–194; IV/3.2, 520–54.

15. See Neder, *Participation in Christ*, 16–18.

16. See Barth, *Church Dogmatics*, IV/3.2, 539, 547.

17. See ibid., IV/3.2, 543–48.

dynamic relationship of call and response, in which the Christian is voluntarily united with Christ in will and action, knows the self to be justified and sanctified in Christ, and awakens to his or her genuine humanity.

Two points must be noted here. First, this relationship of encounter is not "participation" in the more traditional senses of the term (whether we are talking about Platonic formulations or patristic and Reformational understandings of real solidarity with the incarnate humanity of Christ by the power of the Holy Spirit).[18] Second, in contrast to these more traditional understandings of participation, Barth's formulations are relentlessly extrinsic,[19] and this studied extrinsicism is famously reflected in Barth's basically Zwinglian and Baptistic view of the sacraments. Thus, in Barth we encounter a deep and profound Christocentrism that is not, at least in the traditional sense of the term, participationist, and this combination issues in a comparatively low ecclesiology. For Barth, while the church is a vital witness to the world, it is not the decisive sphere of salvation.[20]

In contrast to RO and Barth, Mercersburg offers a vision of theology that is both Christocentric and robustly participationist without slighting either. Not surprisingly,

18. Neder, *Participation in Christ*, 45, rightly notes, "Barth certainly uses the traditional language of participation in the divine being, but he infuses that language with new meaning—his actualistic understanding of divine-human communion. He offers an alternative account in which human participation in God occurs not on the level of a cleansing or transformation of human nature . . . but rather as an event of covenant fellowship in which human beings do not become gods, but rather the human beings they were created to be." See also Boersma, *Heavenly Participation*, 128.

19. On this extrinsic character of Barth's spirituality, see Neder, *Participation*, 11–12, 37; Evans, *Imputation and Impartation*, 243–45.

20. See Healy, "Logic of Karl Barth's Ecclesiology," 265.

it is also vigorously sacramental and ecclesial. The church is indeed the body of Christ and sphere of salvation. All this would seem to suggest that the Mercersburg Theology is worth a second look.

THE PROBLEM OF HIERARCHY

We have noted at various points the Mercersburg affinity for hierarchical views of the church and social reality. Nevin seems to have been inclined, by family background and temperament, toward social conservatism, and though Schaff came from a more humble background, his Berlin connection to the aristocratic and politically conservative "Gerlach circle" apparently had a similar result at least initially (as we have seen, Schaff later came to terms with American democracy). We have also seen the lengths to which Nevin in particular went in portraying the church as a hierarchical, top-down entity, and how he echoed the standard mid-nineteenth century anti-revivalist polemic against the full participation of women in the church. It is no accident at all that Nathan Hatch has presented the Mercersburg theologians as standing in opposition to democratization, as hierarchical traditionalists throwing a spanner into the engine of American egalitarianism! And here an uncomfortable question is posed: was the social impulse of Mercersburg of a piece with European Roman Catholic traditionalists such as Joseph de Maistre and other religious social conservatives of the period? This is an important matter, for the potential fruitfulness of the Mercersburg Theology in our own time will likely be limited to the extent that it is tied too closely to a particular social agenda.

It is at least worth asking, however, whether this Mercersburg attachment to hierarchy was fully consistent with its foundational theological principles. Or was it perhaps simply epiphenomenal and reflective more of the mid-nineteenth century social context and conflicts? We noted in Chapter Six that Nevin's keen interest in an external, mechanical ministerial succession stood in some tension with his concern for the organic, the inward, and the concrete. Here we may go a step further and ask whether this Mercersburg hierarchicalism was fully consistent with the Mercersburg Christocentrism. In this connection we may recall Nevin's argument that Christ has identified himself with and incarnationally united himself with the human race: "Christ must be of the same length and breadth in all respects with humanity as a whole, in order to be at all a real and true Mediator."[21] Perhaps the social implications of Nevin's Christology were grasped more fully, not only by the later Schaff, but also by another European visitor to America, Alexis de Tocqueville, who wrote: "All the great writers of antiquity were a part of the aristocracy of masters, or at least they saw that aristocracy as established without dispute before their eyes; their minds, after expanding in several directions, were therefore found limited in that one, and it was necessary that Jesus Christ come to earth to make it understood that all members of the human species are naturally alike and equal."[22]

QUESTIONS

1. In what ways might Mercersburg's philosophical idealism actually be an asset in our contemporary context?

2. Is Mercersburg's participatory Christocentrism unique in today's theological environment?

21. Nevin, "Noel on Baptism," 249 (MTSS VI, 99).
22. Tocqueville, *Democracy in America*, 413.

3. What lessons might Mercersburg offer to an Evangelical Catholicism today?

BIBLIOGRAPHY

Ahlstrom, Sydney E. "The Scottish Philosophy and American Theology." *Church History* 24 (1955) 257–72.

Appel, Theodore. *The Life and Work of John Williamson Nevin.* Philadelphia: Reformed Church, 1889.

Aubert, Annette. *The German Roots of Nineteenth-Century American Theology.* New York: Oxford University Press, 2017.

Barth, Karl. *Church Dogmatics.* 4 vols. Edited by G. W. Bromiley and T. F. Torrance. Edinburgh: T. & T. Clark, 1936–1969.

———. "Foreword." In Heinrich Heppe, *Reformed Dogmatics: Set Out and Illustrated from the Sources*, edited by Ernst Bizer, v–vii. Translated by G. T. Thomson. London: Allen & Unwin, 1950.

Baxter, Richard. *The Reformed Pastor; or, The Duty of Personal Labors for the Souls of Men.* New York: American Tract Society, n.d.

Bierma, Lyle D. *German Calvinism in the Confessional Age: The Covenant Theology of Caspar Olevianus.* Grand Rapids: Baker, 1996.

Billings, J. Todd. *Calvin, Participation, and the Gift: The Activity of Believers in Union with Christ.* Changing Paradigms in Historical and Systematic Theology. Oxford: Oxford University Press, 2008.

Binkley, Luther J. *The Mercersburg Theology.* Franklin and Marshall College Studies 7. Lancaster, PA: Franklin and Marshall College, 1953.

Boersma, Hans. *Heavenly Participation: The Weaving of a Sacramental Tapestry.* Grand Rapids: Eerdmans, 2011.

Bomberger, J. H. A. *Reformed, not Ritualistic.* Philadelphia: Rodgers, 1867.

———. *The Revised Liturgy: A History and Criticism of the Ritualistic Movement in the German Reformed Church.* Philadelphia: Rodgers, 1867.

Bozeman, Theodore Dwight. *Protestants in an Age of Science: The Baconian Ideal and Ante-bellum American Religious Thought.* Chapel Hill: University of North Carolina Press, 1977.

Braaten, Carl E., and Robert W. Jensen, eds. *Union with Christ: The New Finnish Interpretation of Luther.* Grand Rapids: Eerdmans, 1998.

Brenner, Francis Scott. "Nevin and the Mercersburg Theology." *Theology Today* 12 (1955) 43–56.

Bruce, Robert. *The Mystery of the Lord's Supper: Sermons on the Sacrament Preached in the Kirk of Edinburgh in A.D. 1589.* Translated and edited by Thomas F. Torrance. Edinburgh: Clarke, 1958.

Caldwell, Patricia. *The Puritan Conversion Narrative: The Beginnings of American Expression.* Cambridge: Cambridge University Press, 1983.

Calvin, John. *The Commentaries of John Calvin.* Edinburgh: Calvin Translation Society, 1844–1856. Reprint, Grand Rapids: Eerdmans, 1948–1950.

———. *Institutes of the Christian Religion.* Edited by John T. McNeill. Translated by Ford Lewis Battles. 2 vols. Philadelphia: Westminster, 1960.

Canlis, Julie. *Calvin's Ladder: A Spiritual Theology of Ascent and Ascension.* Grand Rapids: Eerdmans, 2010.

Carlough, William L. "A Historical Comparison of the Theology of John Williamson Nevin and Contemporary Protestant Sacramentalism." PhD diss., New York University, 1961.

Carter, Craig A. *Interpreting Scripture with the Great Tradition: Recovering the Genius of Premodern Exegesis.* Grand Rapids: Baker Academic, 2018.

Conser, Walter H., Jr. *Church and Confession: Conservative Theologians in Germany, England, and America, 1815–1866.* Macon, GA: Mercer University Press, 1984.

Cross, Whitney R. *The Burned-Over District: The Social and Intellectual History of Enthusiastic Religion in Western New York, 1800–1850.* Ithaca, NY: Cornell University Press, 1950.

DeBie, Linden J. *Speculative Theology and Common-Sense Religion: Mercersburg and the Conservative Roots of American Religion.* Princeton Theological Monograph Series 92. Eugene, OR: Pickwick Publications, 2008.

DiPuccio, William. *The Interior Sense of Scripture: The Sacred Hermeneutics of John W. Nevin.* Studies in American Biblical Hermeneutics 14. Macon, GA: Mercer University Press, 1998.

———. "Nevin's Idealist Philosophy." In *Reformed Confessionalism in Nineteenth-Century America: Essays on the Thought of John Williamson Nevin*, edited by Sam Hamstra Jr. and Ari J. Griffioen, 43–67. ATLA Monograph Series 38. Lanham, MD: Scarecrow, 1995.

Dorner, I. A. *The Liturgical Conflict in the Reformed Church of North America, with Special Reference to Fundamental Evangelical Doctrines.* Philadelphia: Loag, 1868. [Also published in *The Reformed Church Monthly* 1 (1868) 327–81.]

Erb, William H., ed. *Dr. Nevin's Theology: Based on Manuscript Class-Room Lectures.* Reading, PA: Beaver, 1913.

Evans, William B. "Calvin's Doctrine of the Lord's Supper and Its Relevance for Today." *Foundations* 68 (May 2015) 4–25.

———. *Imputation and Impartation: Union with Christ in American Reformed Theology.* Milton Keynes, UK: Paternoster, 2008.

———. "Mercersburg and the Reformation: Continuities, Discontinuities, and Lessons to Be Learned." *The New Mercersburg Review* 57 (2017) 20–41.

———. "The Mercersburg Christology and Reformed *Ressourcement.*" *Theology Today* 71 (1015) 393–403.

———. "'Really Exhibited and Conferred . . . in His Appointed Time': Baptism and the New Reformed Sacramentalism." *Presbyterion* 31 (2005) 72–88.

———. "A Tale of Two Pieties: Nurture and Conversion in American Christianity." *Reformation and Revival Journal* 13/3 (2004) 61–75.

———. "Twin Sons of Different Mothers: The Remarkable Theological Convergence of John W. Nevin and Thomas F. Torrance." *Haddington House Journal* 11 (2009) 155–73.

Finney, Charles G. *Lectures on Revivals of Religion.* Boston: Jewett, 1858.

Garcia, Mark A. *Life in Christ: Union with Christ and Twofold Grace in Calvin's Theology.* Eugene, OR: Wipf & Stock, 2008.

Gerhart, Emanuel V. "The Efficacy of Baptism." *Mercersburg Review* 10 (January 1858) 1–44.

———. "The Efficacy of Baptism." In *Born of Water and the Spirit: Essays on the Sacraments and Christian Formation*, edited by David W. Layman, 161–91. Mercersburg Theology Study Series 6. Eugene, OR: Wipf & Stock, 2016.

———. *Institutes of the Christian Religion.* 2 vols. New York: Armstrong, Funk & Wagnalls, 1891, 1894.

———. "Mercersburg Theology." In *The New Schaff-Herzog Encyclopedia of Religious Knowledge*, edited by S. M. Jackson, 7:311–12.
13 vols. New York: Funk & Wagnalls, 1908–1914.

German Reformed Church. *Liturgy for the Use of the Congregations
of the German Reformed Church in the United States of North
America*. Chambersburg, PA: Publication Office of the German
Reformed Church, 1841.

Graham, Stephen R. *Cosmos in the Chaos: Philip Schaff's Interpretation
of Nineteenth-Century American Religion*. Grand Rapids: Eerdmans, 1995.

Grave, S. A. *The Scottish Philosophy of Common Sense*. Oxford: Clarendon, 1960.

Hageman, Howard G. "Back to Mercersburg." *Reformed Journal*
(August 1985) 6.

———. *Pulpit and Table: Some Chapters in the History of Worship in
the Reformed Churches*. Richmond: John Knox, 1962.

Hambrick-Stowe, Charles E. *The Practice of Piety: Puritan Devotional
Disciplines in Seventeenth-Century New England*. Published for
the Institute of Early American History and Culture, Williams-
burg, Virginia. Chapel Hill: University of North Carolina Press,
1982.

Hart, D. G. *John Williamson Nevin: High Church Calvinist*. American
Reformed Biographies 2. Phillipsburg, NJ: P&R, 2005.

Hatch, Nathan O. *The Democratization of American Christianity*. New
Haven: Yale University Press, 1989.

Healy, Nicholas M. "The Logic of Karl Barth's Ecclesiology." *Modern
Theology* 10/3 (1994) 253–70.

Heimert, Alan, and Perry Miller. "Introduction." In *The Great
Awakening: Documents Illustrating the Crisis and Its Consequences*,
edited by Alan Heimert and Perry Miller, xiii–lxi. The American
Heritage Series 34. Indianapolis: Bobbs-Merrill, 1967.

Hodgson, Peter C. "Georg Wilhelm Friedrich Hegel." In *Nineteenth
Century Religious Thought in the West*, edited by Ninian Smart
et al., 1:81–119. 3 vols. Cambridge: Cambridge University Press,
1985.

Holifield, E. Brooks. *The Gentlemen Theologians: American Theology
in Southern Culture, 1795–1860*. Durham: Duke University Press,
1978.

Hunsinger, George. "The Dimension of Depth: Thomas F. Torrance
on the Sacraments of Baptism and the Lord's Supper." *Scottish
Journal of Theology* 54 (2001) 155–76.

Bibliography

Irenaeus. *Against Heresies*. In *The Ante-Nicene Fathers*, edited by Alexander Roberts and James Donaldson, 1:315–567. Reprint, Grand Rapids: Eerdmans, 1981.

Layman, David W. "General Introduction." In *Born of Water and the Spirit: Essays on the Sacraments and Christian Formation*, edited by David W. Layman, 1–33. Mercersburg Theology Study Series 6. Eugene, OR: Wipf & Stock, 2016.

Littlejohn, W. Bradford. *The Mercersburg Theology and the Quest for Reformed Catholicity*. Eugene, OR: Pickwick Publications, 2009.

———. "The Search for Visible Catholicity and the Danger of Boundary-Drawing: Lessons from John Nevin and Richard Hooker." In *Marking the Church: Essays in Ecclesiology*, edited by Greg Peters and Matt Jenson, 122–37. Eugene, OR: Pickwick Publications, 2016.

Loetscher, Lefferts A. *Facing the Enlightenment and Pietism: Archibald Alexander and the Founding of Princeton Theological Seminary*. Contributions to the Study of Religion 8. Presbyterian Historical Society Publications 21. Westport, CT: Greenwood, 1983.

Luther, Martin. *Martin Luther Bondage of the Will*. Translated by J. I. Packer and O. R. Johnston. Cambridge: James Clarke, 1957.

Maxwell, Jack Martin. *Worship and Reformed Theology: The Liturgical Lessons of Mercersburg*. Pittsburgh Theological Monographs Series 10. Pittsburgh: Pickwick Publications, 1976.

McCloy, Frank Dixon. "The Founding of Protestant Theological Seminaries in the United States, 1770–1840." PhD diss., Harvard University, 1959.

Milbank, John, et al. "Suspending the Material: The Turn of Radical Orthodoxy." In *Radical Orthodoxy: A New Theology*, edited by John Milbank et al., 1–20. London: Routledge, 1999.

Miller, Glenn T. *Piety and Intellect: The Aims and Purposes of Ante-Bellum Theological Education*. Scholars Press Studies in Theological Education. Atlanta: Scholars, 1990.

Morgan, Edmund. *Visible Saints: The History of a Puritan Idea*. Ithaca, NY: Cornell University Press, 1963.

Mossner, Ernest Campbell. *The Life of David Hume*. 2nd ed. Oxford: Clarendon, 1980.

Müller, Julius. *The Christian Doctrine of Sin*. Translated by William Pulsford. 2 vols. Clark's Foreign Theological Library 27. Edinburgh: T. & T. Clark, 1852.

Muller, Richard A. "Emanuel V. Gerhart and the 'Christ-Idea' as Fundamental Principle." *Westminster Theological Journal* (1986) 97–117.

Neder, Adam. *Participation in Christ: An Entry into Karl Barth's Church Dogmatics.* Columbia Series in Reformed Theology. Louisville: Westminster John Knox, 2009.

Nevin, John Williamson. "The Anglican Crisis." *Mercersburg Review* 3 (1851) 359–98.

———. *The Anxious Bench.* 2nd ed. Chambersburg, PA: German Reformed Church, 1844.

———. *The Anxious Bench.* 2nd ed. In *Catholic and Reformed: Selected Theological Writings of John Williamson Nevin*, edited by Charles Yrigoyen, Jr. and George H. Bricker, 9–126. Pittsburgh Original Texts & Translations Series 3. Pittsburgh: Pickwick Publications, 1978.

———. *The Anxious Bench.* 2nd ed. In *The Anxious Bench, Antichrist, and the Sermon on Catholic Unity*, edited by Augustine Thompson. Eugene, OR: Wipf & Stock, 2000.

———. "The Apostles' Creed." *Mercersburg Review* 1 (1849) 105–27, 201–21, 313–47.

———. "Catholic Unity." In *The Principle of Protestantism*, by Philip Schaff, 193–215. Chambersburg, PA: German Reformed Church, 1845.

———. "Catholic Unity." In *The Mercersburg Theology*, edited by James Hastings Nichols, 33–55. New York: Oxford University Press, 1966.

———. "Catholic Unity." In *The Anxious Bench, Antichrist, and the Sermon on Catholic Unity*, edited by Augustine Thompson, OP. Eugene, OR: Wipf & Stock, 2000.

———. "Catholicism." *Mercersburg Review* 3 (1851) 1–26.

———. "Catholicism." In *One, Holy, Catholic, and Apostolic, Tome 2: John Nevin's Writings on Ecclesiology (1851–1858)*, edited by Sam Hamstra Jr., 11–32. Mercersburg Theology Study Series 7. Eugene, OR: Wipf & Stock, 2017.

———. *Catholic and Reformed: Selected Theological Writings of John Williamson Nevin*, edited by Charles Yrigoyen, Jr. and George H. Bricker. Pittsburgh Original Texts & Translations Series 3. Pittsburgh: Pickwick Publications, 1979.

———. "*Cur Deus Homo.*" *Mercersburg Review* 3 (1851) 220–39.

———. "*Cur Deus Homo.*" In *The Incarnate Word: Selected Writings on Christology*, edited by William B. Evans, 113–35. Mercersburg Theology Study Series 4. Eugene, OR: Wipf & Stock, 2014.

———. "The Christian Ministry." *Mercersburg Review* 7 (1855) 68–115.

———. "The Christian Ministry." In *One, Holy, Catholic, and Apostolic, Tome Two: John Nevin's Writings on Ecclesiology (1851–1858)*, edited by Sam Hamstra Jr., 38–56. Mercersburg Theology Study Series 7. Eugene, OR: Wipf & Stock, 2017.

———. "The Church." In *The Mercersburg Theology*, edited by James Hastings Nichols, 57–76. New York: Oxford University Press, 1966. [Originally published in 1847.]

———. "Cyprian." *Mercersburg Review* 4 (1852) 259–77, 335–87, 417–52, 513–63.

———. "Doctrine of the Reformed Church on the Lord's Supper." In *The Mystical Presence, and Other Writings on the Eucharist*, edited by Bard Thompson and George H. Bricker, 267–401. Philadelphia: United Church, 1966.

———. "Doctrine of the Reformed Church on the Lord's Supper." In *The Mystical Presence and The Doctrine of the Reformed Church on the Lord's Supper*, edited by Linden J. DeBie, 225–322. Mercersburg Theology Study Series 1. Eugene, OR: Wipf & Stock, 2012.

———. "Early Christianity." *Mercersburg Review* 3 (1851) 461–90, 513–62.

———. "Early Christianity." *Mercersburg Review* 4 (1852) 1–55.

———. "Early Christianity." In *Catholic and Reformed: Selected Theological Writings of John Williamson Nevin*, edited by Charles Yrigoyen Jr. and George H. Bricker, 177–310. Pittsburgh Original Texts & Translations Series 3. Pittsburgh: Pickwick, 1978.

———. "Hodge on the Ephesians." *Mercersburg Review* 9 (1857) 46–83, 192–245.

———. "Hodge on the Ephesians." In *One, Holy, Catholic, and Apostolic, Tome 2: John Nevin's Writings on Ecclesiology (1851–1858)*, edited by Sam Hamstra, Jr., 62–125. Mercersburg Theology Study Series 7. Eugene, OR: Wipf & Stock, 2017.

———. "The Internal Sense of Holy Scripture." *Reformed Quarterly Review* 1 (1883) 5–39.

———. "Jesus and the Resurrection." *Mercersburg Review* 13 (April 1861) 169–91.

———. "Jesus and the Resurrection." In *The Incarnate Word: Selected Writings on Christology*, edited by William B. Evans, 139–58. Mercersburg Theology Study Series 4. Eugene, OR: Wipf & Stock, 2014.

———. "Liebner's Christology." *Mercersburg Review* 3 (January 1851) 55–73.

———. "Liebner's Christology." In *The Incarnate Word: Selected Writings on Christology*, edited by William B. Evans 91–112. Mercersburg Theology Study Series 4. Eugene, OR: Wipf and Stock, 2014.

———. *Life and Character of Frederick Augustus Rauch, First President of Marshall College: A Eulogy*. Chambersburg, PA: Kieffer, 1859.

———. *My Own Life: The Earlier Years*. Lancaster, PA: Historical Society of the Evangelical and Reformed Church, 1964. [Initially published in serial form in the *Reformed Church Messenger* (March 2—June 22, 1870)]

———. *The Mystical Presence: A Vindication of the Reformed or Calvinistic Doctrine of the Holy Eucharist*. Philadelphia: Lippincott, 1846.

———. *The Mystical Presence, and Other Writings on the Eucharist*. Edited by Bard Thompson and George H. Bricker. Lancaster Series on the Mercersburg Theology 4. Philadelphia: United Church, 1966.

———. *The Mystical Presence, and The Doctrine of the Reformed Church on the Lord's Supper*. Edited by Linden J. DeBie. Mercersburg Theology Study Series 1. Eugene, OR: Wipf & Stock, 2012.

———. "Noel on Baptism." *Mercersburg Review* (May 1850) 231–65.

———. "Noel on Baptism." In *Born of Water and the Spirit: Essays on the Sacraments and Christian Formation*, edited by David W. Layman 83–115. Mercersburg Theology Study Series 6. Eugene, OR: Wipf and Stock, 2016.

———. *One, Holy, Catholic, and Apostolic, Tome 1: John Nevin's Writings on Ecclesiology (1844–1849)*. Edited by Sam Hamstra, Jr. Mercersburg Theology Study Series 5. Eugene, OR: Wipf and Stock, 2017.

———. *One, Holy, Catholic, and Apostolic, Tome 2: John Nevin's Writings on Ecclesiology (1851–1858)*. Edited by Sam Hamstra, Jr. Mercersburg Theology Study Series 7. Eugene, OR: Wipf and Stock, 2017.

———. "Preliminary Notice to the Second Edition." In Frederick A. Rauch, *Psychology: Or, A View of the Human Soul, Including Anthropology*, vii–ix. 4th ed. New York: Dodd, 1853.

———. "Puritanism and the Creed." *Mercersburg Review* 1 (November 1849) 585–607.

———. "Review of *God in Christ*." *Mercersburg Review* 1 (1849) 311–12.

———. "The Sect System." *Mercersburg Review* 1 (1849) 482–507, 521–39.

———. "The Sect System." In *Catholic and Reformed: Selected Theological Writings of John Williamson Nevin*, edited by Charles Yrigoyen, Jr. and George H. Bricker, 128–73. Pittsburgh Original Texts & Translations Series 3. Pittsburgh: Pickwick, 1978.

———. *A Summary of Biblical Antiquities; for the Use of Schools, Bible-Classes and Families.* Philadelphia: American Sunday-School Union, 1849.

———. "True and False Protestantism," *Mercersburg Review* 1 (January 1849) 83–104.

———. *Vindication of the Revised Liturgy, Historical, and Theological.* In *Catholic and Reformed: Selected Theological Writings of John Williamson Nevin*, edited by Charles Yrigoyen Jr. and George H. Bricker, 313–403. 1867. Reprint, Pittsburgh Original Texts & Translations Series 3. Pittsburgh: Pickwick, 1978.

Nevin, John Williamson, and Charles Hodge. *Coena Mystica: Debating Reformed Eucharistic Theology.* Edited by Linden J. DeBie. Mercersburg Theology Study Series 2. Eugene, OR: Wipf & Stock, 2013.

Nevin, John Williamson, Philip Schaff, and Daniel Gans. *The Incarnate Word: Selected Writings on Christology.* Edited by William B. Evans. Mercersburg Theology Study Series 4. Eugene, OR: Wipf & Stock, 2014.

Nevin, John Williamson, Philip Schaff, and Emanuel V. Gerhart. *Born of Water and the Spirit: Essays on the Sacraments and Christian Formation.* Edited by David W. Layman. Mercersburg Theology Study Series 6. Eugene, OR: Wipf & Stock, 2016.

Nichols, James Hastings, ed. *The Mercersburg Theology.* A Library of Protestant Thought. New York: Oxford University Press, 1966.

———. *Romanticism in American Theology: Nevin and Schaff at Mercersburg.* Chicago: University of Chicago Press, 1961.

Owens, L. Roger. *The Shape of Participation: A Theology of Church Practices.* Eugene, OR: Cascade Books, 2010.

Plummer, Kenneth Moses. "The Theology of John Williamson Nevin in the Mercersburg Period, 1840–1852." PhD diss., University of Chicago, 1858.

Rauch, Frederick A. *Psychology: Or, A View of the Human Soul, Including Anthropology,* 4th ed. New York: Dodd, 1853.

Richards, George Warren. "The Mercersburg Theology, Historically Considered." *Papers of the American Society of Church History,* 2nd ser., 3 (1912) 119–49

———. "The Mercersburg Theology: Its Purpose and Principles." *Church History* 20 (1951) 42–55.

Schaff, David. *The Life of Philip Schaff: In Part Autobiographical.* New York: Scribner, 1897.

Schaff, Philip. *America: A Sketch of the Political, Social, and Religious Character of the United State of North America.* New York: Scribner, 1855.

———. *The Anglo-American Sabbath.* New York: American Tract Society, 1863.

———. *Church and State in the United States.* New York: Scribner, 1888.

———. *The Creeds of Christendom, with a History and Critical Notes.* 3 vols. New York: Harper & Brothers, 1877.

———. *The Development of the Church: The Principle of Protestantism and other Historical Writings of Philip Schaff.* Edited by David R. Bains and Theodore Louis Trost. The Mercersburg Theology Study Series 3. Eugene, OR: Wipf & Stock, 2017.

———. *Germany; Its Universities, Theology, and Religion.* Philadelphia: Lindsay & Blakiston, 1857.

———. *History of the Apostolic Church with a General Introduction to Church History.* Translated by Edward D. Yeomans. New York: Scribner, 1854.

———. *History of the Christian Church.* 3rd rev. ed. 7 vols. New York: Scribner, 1890.

———. *In Memoriam: Our Children in Heaven.* New York: privately printed, 1876.

———. "Introduction" In Emanuel V. Gerhart, *Institutes of the Christian Religion,* I:xi–xv. 2 vols. New York: Armstrong, Funk & Wagnalls, 1891, 1894.

———. *The Moral Character of Christ, or the Perfection of Christ's Humanity a Proof of His Divinity.* Chambersburg, PA: Kieffer, 1861.

———. *The Principle of Protestantism.* Lancaster Series on the Mercersburg Theology 1. Philadelphia: United Church, 1964.

———. *The Principle of Protestantism.* Chambersburg, PA: German Reformed Church, 1845.

———. *The Principle of Protestantism.* In *The Development of the Church: The Principle of Protestantism, and other Historical Writings of Philip Schaff,* edited by David R. Bains and Theodore Louis Trost, 35–205. Mercersburg Theology Study Series 3. Eugene, OR: Wipf & Stock, 2017.

———. *Reformed and Catholic: Selected Historical and Theological Writings of Philip Schaff.* Edited by Charles Yrigoyen Jr. and George H. Bricker. Pittsburgh: Pickwick Publications, 1979.

———. *Theological Propadeutic: A General Introduction to the Study of Theology: Exegetical, Historical, Systematic, and Practical.* New York: Scribner, 1892.

———. *What Is Church History: A Vindication of the Idea of Historical Development.* Philadelphia: Lippincott, 1846.

Schleiermacher, Friedrich. *The Christian Faith.* Edited by H. R. Mackintosh and J. S. Stewart. Edinburgh: T. & T. Clark, 1928.

Shriver, George H. *Philip Schaff: Christian Scholar and Ecumenical Prophet.* Macon, GA: Mercer University Press, 1987.

Smith, James K. A. "Will the Real Plato Please Stand Up? Participation versus Incarnation." In *Radical Orthodoxy and the Reformed Tradition,* 61–72. Edited by James K. A. Smith and James H. Olthuis. Grand Rapids: Baker, 2005.

Smith, Norman Kemp. *The Philosophy of David Hume: A Critical Study of Its Origins and Central Doctrines.* London: Macmillan, 1960.

Steinmetz, David. "The Superiority of Pre-Critical Exegesis." *Theology Today* 37 (1980) 27–38.

Taylor, Nathaniel William. "*Concio ad Clerum:* A Sermon on Human Nature, Sin, and Freedom." In *Theology in America: The Major Protestant Voices from Puritanism to Neo-Orthodoxy,* 213–49. Edited by Sydney E. Ahlstrom. Indianapolis: Bobbs-Merrill, 1967. [Originally published as *Concio ad Clerum. A Sermon Delivered in the Chapel of Yale College, September 10, 1828.* New Haven: Hezekiah Howe, 1828.]

Tocqueville, Alexis de. *Democracy in America.* Translated and edited by Harvey C. Mansfield and Delba Winthrop. Chicago: University of Chicago Press, 2000.

Torrance, Thomas F. "Karl Barth and the Latin Heresy." *Scottish Journal of Theology* 39 (1986) 461–82.

Tracy, David W. "The Catholic Analogical Imagination." *Proceedings of the Catholic Theological Society of America* (1977) 234–44.

Ullmann, Carl. "Preliminary Essay." In *The Mystical Presence: A Vindication of the Reformed or Calvinistic Doctrine of the Holy Eucharist,* by John W. Nevin, 13–47. Philadelphia: J. B. Lippincott, 1846. [A loose translation of Ullmann's "Das Wesen des Christentums." *Studien und Kritiken* (1845); Also published in *The Mystical Presence and The Doctrine of the Reformed Church on the Lord's Supper,* 15–39. Edited by Linden J. DeBie.

The Mercersburg Theology Study Series 1. Eugene, OR: Wipf & Stock, 2012.]

Wallace, R. S. *Calvin's Doctrine of Word and Sacrament*. Grand Rapids: Eerdmans, 1957.

Weber, Otto. *Foundations of Dogmatics*. Translated by Darrell L. Guder. 2 vols. Grand Rapids: Eerdmans, 1981.

Wentz, Richard E. *John Williamson Nevin: American Theologian*. New York: Oxford University Press, 1997.

Wolff, B. C. "German Reformed Dogmatics." *Mercersburg Review* 9 (1857) 249–72; *Mercersburg Review* 10 (1858) 58–83. [A "free translation" of a portion of Ebrard's *Christliche Dogmatik*.]

Yoder, Don. "The Bench versus The Catechism: Revivalism and Pennsylvania's Lutheran and Reformed Churches." *Pennsylvania Folklife* 10 (Fall 1959) 14–23.

Yrigoyen, Charles, Jr. "Emanuel V. Gerhart and the Mercersburg Theology." PhD diss., Temple University, 1973.

———. "Emanuel V. Gerhart: Apologist for the Mercersburg Theology." *Journal of Presbyterian History* 57 (1979) 485–500.

———. "Mercersburg's Quarrel with Methodism." In *Rethinking Methodist History: A Bicentennial Historical Consultation*, edited by Russell E. Richey and Kenneth E. Rowe, 194–203. Nashville: Kingswood, 1985.

Ziegler, Howard J. B. *Frederick Augustus Rauch: American Hegelian*. Lancaster, PA: Franklin and Marshall College, 1953.

Zwingli, Ulrich. "On the Lord's Supper." In *Zwingli and Bullinger*, 185–238. Edited by G. W. Bromiley. Philadelphia: Westminster, 1953.

INDEX

Index